Vacation
CRAFTING

Vacation CRAFTING

150+ SUMMER CAMP PROJECTS FOR BOYS & GIRLS TO MAKE

Suzanne McNeill

Happy Fox BOOKS

CONTENTS

LOOK WHAT YOU CAN MAKE!

10

FOAM

68

FRIENDSHIP BRACELETS

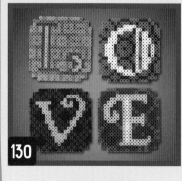

130

FUSIBLE BEADS

INTRODUCTION

ARE YOU READY FOR A CRAFTY VACATION?

Getting away from it all doesn't have to mean getting away from entertaining craft projects! Even during the most exciting school breaks, you sometimes have an hour—or a whole afternoon—with nothing to do. The fast, fun crafts in this book are perfect whether you're enjoying a summer afternoon at the kitchen table or you're away from home without all your usual art supplies. You only need easy-to-pack or inexpensive materials available almost anywhere you'll be vacationing. These crafts can fill your downtime with inspiration and enjoyment for your entire family. And if you only have an hour free here and there, don't worry—most of these projects work just

fine if you start them, put them down, and pick them up again later in the day.

So, let's get started! Use craft foam, seashells, or pretty string to make decorations for your room. Deck yourself out in hemp jewelry and make friendship bracelets for your besties. Practice your plastic lace skills on lanyards and your rubber band skills on cell phone cases. Make some pony bead animals and try your hand at tie-dye. From duct tape to fusible beads, there's something here for everyone. It's time for vacation—and time to get crafty!

MATERIALS AND SKILLS

A QUICK LOOK AT WHAT YOU MIGHT NEED!

There is such a variety of projects in this book that it would be impossible to list all the materials, tools, and skills you'd need for all of them in one place. Luckily for you, virtually every item to make every project in this book is available at large craft stores. If you're at home, you'll probably have some of the basics like scissors and glue on hand already. But if you're going on a trip, you'll want to make sure you look at the specific projects you want to make before you go so that you can bring along the materials and tools you'll need. Some projects do require quite particular materials or tools that you might have trouble finding at the beach or deep in the woods! Read on to get an idea of the general materials you'll need for each of the sections in this book.

FOAM: Foam crafts are all about what you add to the foam and what you add the foam to! You'll need **craft foam**, which is available in a ton of colors, and then **miscellaneous materials** that can usually all be found at the craft store, like wood craft sticks, wiggle eyes, glitter glue, chenille stems, and more. Technique-wise, it's usually as simple as cutting and gluing!

SEASHELLS: You can either **purchase shells** or use **shells you've collected yourself** during a sandy day at the beach. Speaking of sandy, be sure to wipe or wash your shells well before you start crafting with them to make sure the adhesive stays stuck! Since shells can be heavy and textured, it's best to use **hot glue** or a heavy-duty glue like **E6000** to glue shell projects.

STRING: You can use **embroidery floss** and **craft thread** for a surprising number of crafts! From funky string art to classic dream catchers, you usually don't need much more than some kind of base material like a wooden plaque or a plastic canvas to make string projects.

HEMP: Knots are what make hemp projects come together! In general, all you need is **hemp** and the knowledge of a few basic knots to create some magical jewelry. You can also incorporate **beads** of any stripe into a hemp project. Hemp can be a good project to take in the car. See the notes for friendship bracelets, below, for more of what you might need.

Almost every project in this book requires a pair of scissors, a ruler, or both. So make sure you don't leave the house without them! (They're not listed in the individual materials lists.)

FRIENDSHIP BRACELETS: For any friendship bracelet project, you just need two things: **embroidery floss** and something to hold the bracelet down while you work! This can be tape, a safety pin, a heavy stack of books, or even something sticking out from a surface in the car or on a desk that you can loop the bracelet around. Wherever you are, you are sure to be able to whip your thread out of your pocket and get knotting.

PLASTIC LACE: Much like making hemp and friendship bracelets, you basically only need **plastic lace** and something to hold your project down while you work. You may want to incorporate **lanyard hooks** or **key rings** when making some projects. All the projects in this book use the flat kind of plastic lace, not the round kind. You can experiment with the round kind if you want, but most of the projects will look quite different with round lace, and some may not really work.

RUBBER BANDS: To make the rubber band projects in this book, you'll need one or two **rubber band looms**, such as a Rainbow Loom™, plus the **hook** that comes with the loom. To make your life easier, you probably will also want the little **plastic clips** that come with loom kits and rubber bands, though you can use other found materials like paper clips if you need to. Other than that, all you have to buy is a collection of cute little **rubber bands** in all your favorite colors!

PONY BEADS: You'll be amazed at how quickly projects made with **pony beads** come together! For most pony bead projects, you'll need some kind of **cord**, like plastic lace, hemp, yarn, elastic, or really anything. You'll also often need glue.

FUSIBLE BEADS: There are many brands of **fusible beads** out there, such as Perler Beads®, but they all pretty much work the same way—use a **hot iron** to melt them together! You'll need special plastic **pegboards** (in various shapes) to create and hold together the designs you make, plus **protective ironing paper** like parchment paper. Be careful or get help from an adult when using the hot iron. Tweezers can be helpful for picking up and placing beads, but aren't essential.

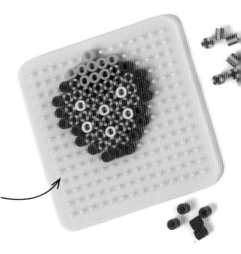

TiE-DYE: Get ready to get messy with tie-dye projects! Besides the **dye**, **water**, **buckets**, and other materials, you'll want to make sure you are wearing **clothes** that you don't mind getting a bit stained, and you should probably grab some **rubber or plastic gloves** to avoid staining your hands, too. There's a lot more info about materials in the tie-dye section.

DUCT TAPE: To get the most out of **duct tape**, you'll need a **cutting mat** and a **craft knife** to make clean cuts and keep your duct tape sticky. Be careful or get help from an adult when using a craft knife. You can also use scissors to make many cuts.

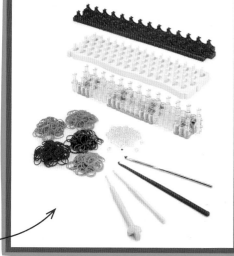

LADYBUG VISOR

Clever and cute, this ladybug will complete your super summer look.

MATERIALS

- 4" (10cm)-wide red foam visor
- Black permanent marker
- 1 black chenille stem
- 2 wiggle eyes
- ⅛" (0.3cm) hole punch
- Glue

1. Using a black marker, outline the visor edge and draw random circles. Fill in the circles.

2. Glue wiggle eyes in place. Draw eyelashes above the eyes.

3. Punch two holes 2½" (6.5cm) apart into the top rim of the visor. Bend a chenille stem into a U shape, poke both ends up through the holes from the underside to the topside, and curl the antenna ends with your fingers.

DAFFODILS VISOR

Keep the sun off of your face when you're working in the flower garden.

MATERIALS

- 4" (10cm)-wide white foam visor
- Yellow silk daffodils
- White mini brads
- Pushpin

1. Using a pushpin, poke 15 holes evenly along the top rim of the visor.
2. Attach a silk flower to each hole with a brad.
3. Open the legs of each brad on the underside of the visor to secure the flowers in place.

CATERPILLAR VISOR

This bright visor is easy to make, adorable, and will add a touch of whimsy to any outfit!

MATERIALS

- 4" (10cm)-wide green foam visor
- 2 green foam pom-poms
- Adhesive-backed foam sheets in red, green, and light green
- Green permanent marker
- 1 red chenille stem
- 3 lime green chenille stems
- 2 wiggle eyes
- ⅛" (0.3cm) hole punch
- Glitter glue
- Glue

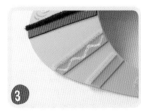

1. Cut adhesive-backed foam sheets into the following ½" (1.5cm)-wide strips: three green, two light green, and two red. Trim them to size and adhere them to the visor.
2. Cut chenille stems to match each strip and adhere them in place.
3. Add a wavy line of glitter glue to some of the strips and let dry.
4. Glue eyes onto the visor. Draw eye details below the eyes with marker.
5. Punch two holes 2" (5cm) apart into the top rim of the visor. Bend a green chenille stem into a U shape and poke both ends up through the holes from the underside to the topside.
6. Push a foam pom-pom onto each end of the chenille stem and bend the stem to make the antennae curve.

FiRECRACKER HAT

This fits-any-size hat is just the thing to celebrate the 4th of July, Veteran's Day, or any holiday that could use some sparkle and pizzazz. If you don't live in the United States, adjust the colors and lettering to reflect your own country.

MATERIALS

- 9" x 12" (23 x 30.5cm) foam sheets in red, white, and blue
- 12" x 18" (30.5 x 45.5cm) foam sheet in black
- 1" (2.5cm) foam glitter sticker letters
- 3 gold metallic chenille stems
- 3 glitter 1¼" (3cm) pom-poms
- 3 wood 2½" (6.5cm) craft sticks
- Gold glitter dimensional paint
- Acrylic paint in red, white, and blue
- Paintbrush

1. Cut a candle out of red, white, and blue foam and slightly round the corners with scissors. Cut a star out of red and blue foam. Cut a strip of black foam that is 1¼" (3cm) wide and long enough to fit comfortably around the head of the wearer with a little bit of overlap.
2. Glue pom-poms onto the chenille stems, then glue the chenille stems onto the backs of the candles.
3. Paint one craft stick in each color. When dry, glue one stick to the back of each candle to act as a support.
4. Glue the ends of black headband strip together. Glue the firecrackers to the front of the headband. Press on the glitter letters. Outline the stars with gold glitter paint and glue them on the hat.

Photocopy at 200%

Candle

Star

Photocopy at 200%

LiME FUN FRAME

Quick, easy, and fun, rub-ons provide endless possibilities for giving a frame its own unique style.

MATERIALS

- Lime foam frame
- Rub-on flower designs
- Blue and green adhesive-backed rhinestones
- 28" (71cm) of green ribbon, ⅜" (1cm) wide
- ⅛" (0.3cm) hole punch

1. Apply rub-on flowers as desired to the entire frame. Don't be afraid to overlap some flowers!
2. Adhere rhinestones to the centers of the flowers.
3. Punch two holes near the top corners of the frame. Thread ribbon through the holes and tie a bow for hanging.

CATERPILLAR FRAME

Foam critters sparkle on this cute frame that is perfect for any fans of creepy-crawlies who love to explore forests and streams.

MATERIALS

- Blue foam frame
- White foam adhesive letters
- Green foam caterpillar
- Green foam dragonfly with blue foam details
- Opal and blue glitter glues
- Black, blue, and white permanent markers
- 4" (10cm) of silver 22-gauge wire
- Wire cutters or old scissors
- Round-nose pliers
- Glue

1. Outline circles on the caterpillar body with marker, alternating white and blue. Draw a smile and antennae. Use glitter glue to accent the body. Glue the caterpillar to the frame.
2. Outline the white letters with blue marker and adhere them to the frame.
3. Cut the wire into two 2" (5cm) pieces. Make antennae by creating a spiral on one end of each wire using round-nose pliers. Poke the other ends directly into the dragonfly's head. Add details to the dragonfly's body, then glue it to the frame.

SHINY FISH

Sequins transform into sparkling fish scales on this clever project for kids who can't get enough of marine motifs.

MATERIALS

- Teal fish foam shape or sheet
- Lime sequins
- Glue
- ⅛" (0.3cm) hole punch

1. If you don't have a pre-made fish shape, cut one out. Punch a hole for the eye.
2. Draw scalloped rows on the fish with glue and apply overlapping lime sequins while the glue is wet. Let dry.

SWIRLY DOLPHIN

You'll have fun drawing the watery swirls on this majestic mammal.

MATERIALS

- Blue dolphin foam shape or sheet
- 1 small wiggle eye
- Opal glitter glue
- Glue

1. If you don't have a pre-made dolphin shape, cut one out.
2. Using opal glitter glue, draw random swirls and squiggles onto the dolphin and let dry.
3. Glue on a single wiggle eye.

GLITTER SEAHORSE

Add some sparkle to your room or under-the-sea-themed party!

MATERIALS

- Teal seahorse foam shape or sheet
- 1 small wiggle eye
- Glitter glues in teal, copper, and purple
- Glue

1. If you don't have a pre-made seahorse shape, cut one out.
2. Apply glitter glue to the seahorse following the design shown and let dry.
3. Glue on a single wiggle eye.

FiNGER PUPPET FAMiLY

Project by Kathy Wegner

Create a story with finger puppets. This is a great activity for a scout meeting. It's also fun if you want to make one to represent each member of your family!

MATERIALS

- Foam sheets/pieces in yellow, blue, green, red, tan, peach, orange, black, dark brown, and light brown—at least 4" x 5" (10 x 12.5cm) for each body
- Permanent markers in black, pink, and red
- 3 white ⅜" (1cm) buttons
- Assorted seed beads
- White dimensional paint
- Glitter glue
- Glue

1. Use the patterns to trace and cut out the body parts you need. Roll the bodies into a tube and glue them together using the tabs. Then push the heads together and glue them in place, closing off the top of the tube.

2. Glue on faces, hair, and arms. Draw facial features with markers.

3. Decorate the bodies with glitter, buttons, and beads.

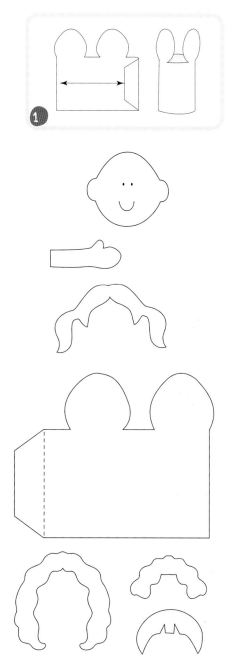

SPORTY SCHEDULE HOLDER

This sports activity magnet is just what you need to keep track of all your games and practices!

MATERIALS

- 12" x 18" (30.5 x 45.5cm) foam sheet in royal blue
- 9" x 12" (23 x 30.5cm) foam sheets in white, cream, light brown, brown, orange, and green
- ⅝" (1.5cm) foam adhesive letters
- 3 wood clip-style 1¾" (4.5cm) clothespins
- 4½" x 13½" (11.5 x 34.5cm) magnetic adhesive sheet
- Black and red permanent markers
- Gold and blue glitter stars (¾"—1½" [2—4cm])

1. Cut the following foam shapes using the patterns: one soccer ball, one baseball, and one set of football stripes from white; one baseball bat from cream; one football from light brown; one basketball from orange; and one sports flag from green. Also cut a 5" x 18" (12.5 x 45.5cm) rectangle from blue foam and a thin strip of brown for the sports flagpole.

2. Draw lines on the balls and bat and a soccer ball pattern on the soccer ball.

3. Glue the brown flagpole onto the flag and add a name with adhesive letters. Glue the white stripes to each end of the football.

4. Glue the magnet sheet to the back of the blue foam. Glue one clothespin in the center front lower edge of the blue foam, then the other two clothespins about 2" (5cm) in from each side.

5. Glue stars to the clothespins as shown, then glue all the sports shapes and more stars to the blue foam.

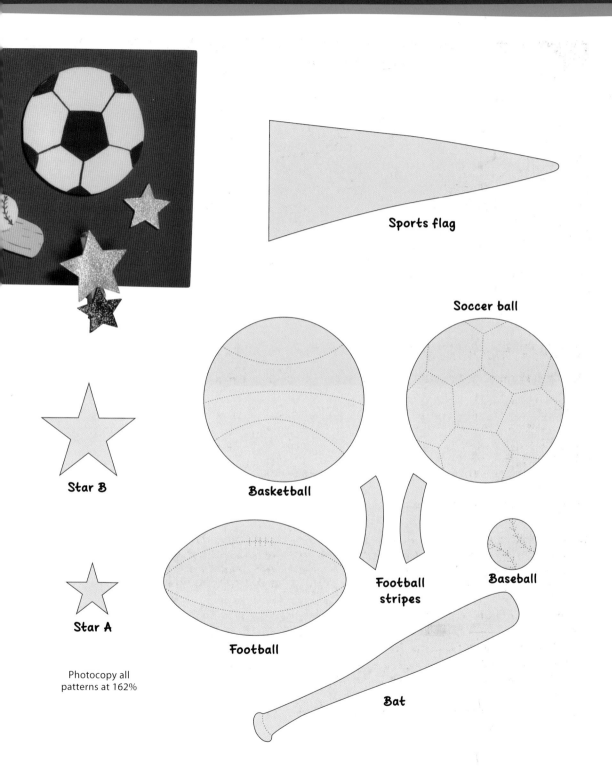

Sports flag

Soccer ball

Star B

Basketball

Star A

Football

Football
stripes

Baseball

Bat

Photocopy all
patterns at 162%

LADYBUG PLACEMAT

Bring ladybugs and dragonflies to the table on this fun placemat. Throw a garden party and make enough for all your guests!

MATERIALS

- 12" x 18" (30.5 x 45.5cm) foam sheet in green
- 9" x 12" (23 x 30.5cm) foam sheets in white, black, and red
- Crystal glitter paint
- Green acrylic paint
- Fine-tipped paintbrush
- 3½" (9cm) of 18-gauge copper wire
- Wire cutters or old scissors
- Needle-nosed pliers

1. Cut the following foam shapes using the patterns: six dragonflies from white; one ladybug body from red; and six thoraxes, one ladybug head, three ladybug spots, and one ladybug stripe from black.

2. Paint the dragonfly wings with glitter paint and dot two green eyes onto the thoraxes. Glue the thoraxes on top of the wings.

3. Use needle-nosed pliers to bend the copper wire into a U shape. Poke one end of the wire into the top of the ladybug head and back up through so that the two ends stick up as antennae. Bend the ends into circles.

4. Glue the ladybug head, stripe, and dots to the ladybug body. Glue the entire ladybug in the center of the placemat. Glue three dragonflies on each side of the ladybug.

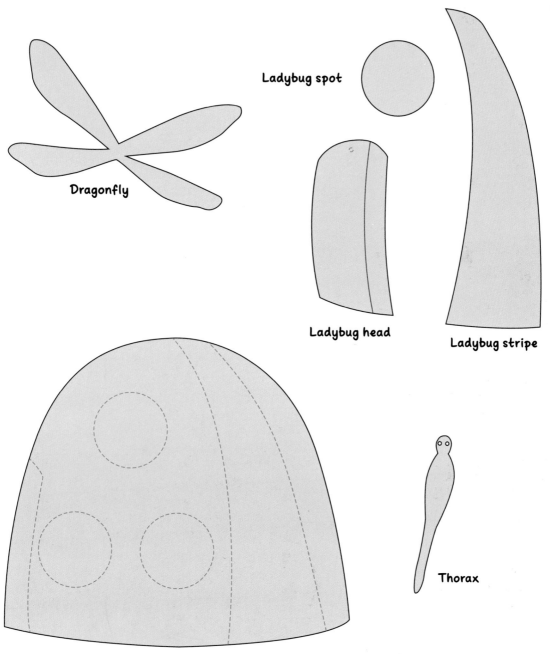

Dragonfly

Ladybug spot

Ladybug head

Ladybug stripe

Ladybug body

Thorax

Photocopy all
patterns at 100%

TROPICAL WINDSOCK

Create a tropical windsock to enjoy yourself or give as a gift. It's a great reminder of how much fun it is to be at the ocean!

MATERIALS

- 12" x 18" (30.5 x 45.5cm) foam sheets in blue, chartreuse green, lavender, and yellow
- 9" x 12" (23 x 30.5cm) foam sheets in dark green, medium green, tan, turquoise, light pink, dark pink, white, orange, and light orange
- Brown and green dimensional paint
- Blue, crystal, and green glitter paint
- Black acrylic paint
- Fine-tipped paintbrush
- Assorted small seashells
- 3 yards (3m) of ¼" (0.5cm) chartreuse green satin ribbon
- ¼" (0.5cm) hole punch

1. Cut the following foam shapes using the patterns: one fins D and one seaweed from dark green; one seaweed from medium green; one sand from tan; one fins C from turquoise; one fish B from light pink; one fins B from dark pink; one each fish eyes A, B, C, and D from white; one fish A from orange; one fins A from light orange; one fish D and one seaweed from chartreuse green; and one fish C from yellow.

2. Cut the following danglers that are 1¼" x 12" (3 x 30.5cm): three from chartreuse green, three from lavender, and three from yellow. From the blue foam, cut one piece that is 7" x 18" (18 x 45.5cm) and four pieces that are ½" x 1½" (1.5 x 4cm).

3. Paint all the details on all the fish parts black. Add details to all the seaweed, using green between adjacent seaweed and green glitter for seaweed veins. Also add brown lines to the sand. Glue the sand and seaweed onto the large blue foam base. Glue seashells onto the sand.

4. Glue all the fins, eyes, and tails to the various fish, then glue the fish to the blue base. Add bubbles of blue paint and crystal glitter dots.

5. Glue danglers evenly around the bottom of the blue base. Then roll the blue base into a tube with a slight overlap and glue in place to create the windsock shape.

6. Use a hole punch to punch four holes spaced evenly around the top rim of the windsock, about ⅜" (1cm) down from the edge. Glue the small blue strips over the holes on the inside, then re-punch the same holes. Cut the ribbon into four equal lengths. Loop a ribbon through each hole. Bring all the loose ends together and tie, leaving 4" (10cm) of ribbon hanging loose. Tie two of the loose ribbons together to create a loop for hanging.

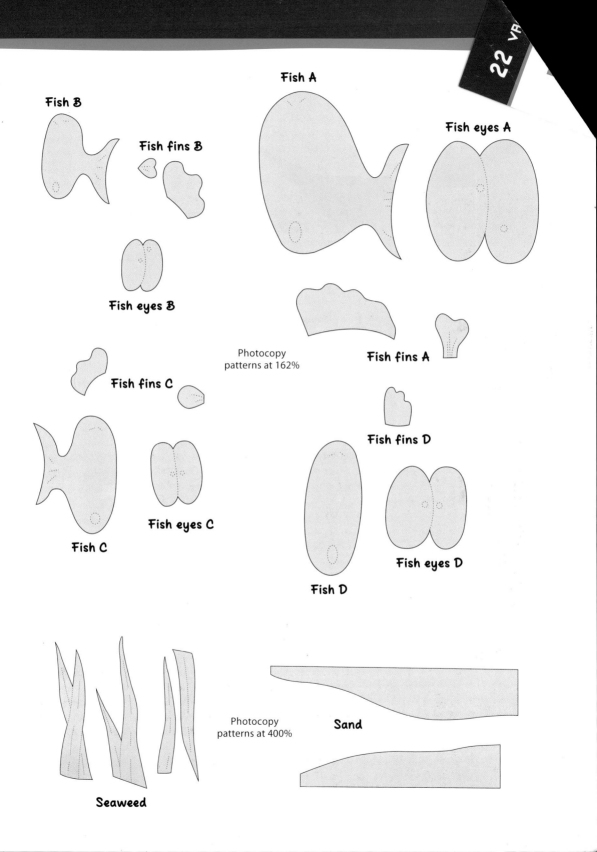

Fish B

Fish A

Fish fins B

Fish eyes A

Fish eyes B

Photocopy
patterns at 162%

Fish fins A

Fish fins C

Fish fins D

Fish C

Fish eyes C

Fish D

Fish eyes D

Photocopy
patterns at 400%

Sand

Seaweed

CARDINAL PLANT POKE

Project by Kathy Wegner

This cardinal will brighten your yard with his dazzling red color.

MATERIALS

- Red and black foam sheets
- 12" (30.5cm) stick or dowel
- 2 black beads
- Black and gold dimensional paint
- Glue

1. Cut out two red cardinal bodies and two black cardinal wings.
2. Glue the dowel between both body pieces. Then glue a wing on each side.
3. Paint the beak gold on both sides. Paint the face area black on both sides. Let dry.
4. Glue a bead on each side for eyes.

ROBIN PLANT POKE

Robins bring spring! But you can enjoy them all season long with this garden decoration.

MATERIALS

- Brown and orange foam sheets
- 12" (30.5cm) stick or dowel
- 2 black beads
- White and gold dimensional paint
- Glue

1. Cut out two brown robin bodies, two brown robin wings, and two orange robin breasts.
2. Glue one breast, one wing, and one bead for an eye on each body piece. Then glue the dowel between both body pieces.
3. Paint the beak gold on both sides. Paint the neck area white on both sides. Let dry.

DRAGONFLY PLANT POKE

Glistening wings add sparkle among your flowers.

MATERIALS

- White and turquoise foam sheets
- 12" (30.5cm) stick or dowel
- Opal and turquoise dimensional paint
- Glue

1. Cut out two white dragonfly wings and two turquoise dragonfly bodies.
2. Glue each body piece to a set of wings. Then glue the dowel between both wing pieces.
3. Add sparkle to the wings and body with dimensional paint.

LADYBUG PLANT POKE

Ladybugs are a welcome guest in any garden!

MATERIALS

- Red and black foam sheets
- 12" (30.5cm) stick or dowel
- Black permanent marker
- Black dimensional paint
- Glue

1. Cut out two black ladybug bodies (with the head and legs) and two red ladybug wings (the round shape).
2. Draw a center line on each wing piece with marker, then add spots with dimensional paint. Glue each wing piece to a body piece.
3. Glue the dowel between both body pieces.

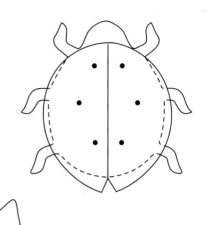

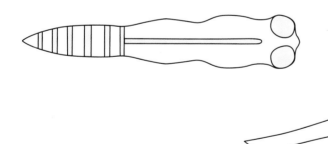

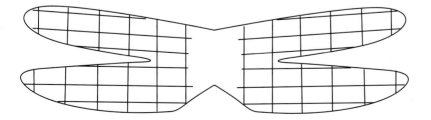

PHOTO ALBUM COVER

Relive the fun! Display your fabulous vacation photos in a photo album that is almost as interesting as the event itself.

MATERIALS

- Green spiral-bound photo album
- Yellow foam photo frame sized to fit album cover
- 3 green foam bugs
- 2 yellow foam bugs
- Pony beads: 10 green, 10 yellow, and 10 gold
- 6 green ¼" (0.5cm)-wide ribbons, 4" (10cm) long
- Green gel pen
- ⅛" (0.3cm) hole punch
- Glue

1. Punch 10 holes across the bottom of the photo frame ½" (1.5cm) apart. Tie a knot in the end of one ribbon, thread the leading ribbon end up through the first hole to the front of the frame, add three beads, and knot the leading end securely. Do this again on the last hole.

2. For the middle eight holes, each ribbon will go through two holes. Knot the end, string on three beads, thread the leading ribbon end down through a hole and back up through the hole next to it to the front of the frame, add three more beads, and knot again.

3. Write words and draw doodles on the frame with a green gel pen. Glue a green bug on one corner. Adhere more bugs to individual pages to form tabs. Glue the frame to the front of the photo album along with your favorite photo.

Raffin' The Pigeon River 06

SEASHELL FRAME

This cool project incorporates not only seashells, but some totally nautical netting as well, for a real down-to-earth effect that works perfectly for a fishing trip or beach adventure.

MATERIALS

- Assorted shells
- 4¾" x 6¾" (12 x 17cm) photo frame
- Light blue-green spray paint
- Blue crackle spray paint
- Matte spray sealer

- 2 yards (2m) of jute twine
- Decorative netting
- Sea glass
- Hot glue

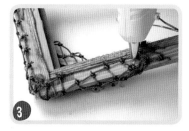

1. Wrap each side of the frame three times with twine. Secure in place with glue.
2. Spray paint the entire frame with several heavy coats of blue-green spray paint and allow to dry. Spray on several heavy coats of blue crackle paint with no drying time between coats. After this paint is dry, spray with a matte sealer and allow to dry.
3. Cut a piece of decorative netting to fit around the corners of the frame. Hot glue in place where there are knots in the net to hide the glue.
4. Glue on sea glass and shells as desired.

GENERAL SEASHELL CRAFTING TIPS

- Since shells are heavy and textured, it's best to use E6000 or hot glue when gluing them, as opposed to regular all-purpose glue. But regular glue can work for some projects.
- Wash and dry shells thoroughly before using them. Brush them vigorously with a sturdy wire brush, then with a toothbrush and water. Glue won't stick to wet shells.
- To trim broken edges of shells, cut them with wire cutters, then smooth the rough edges with a file or sandpaper.
- Whiten discolored sand dollars and shells by soaking them in a solution of 1 part chlorine bleach to 4 parts water. Get an adult's help to handle the bleach.
- Bright sunlight will fade shell colors.
- Finish shell projects with a clear gloss acrylic spray sealer if desired.

UNDER THE SEA BOX

This bright and cute box is large enough to hold all your souvenirs from a sandy vacation, or an entire collection of shells. Pick your favorites to use as the decoration on the top!

MATERIALS

- 3 medium fan shells
- 3 small fan shells
- Assorted shells and starfish
- 8" x 11" (20 x 28cm) blue storage box
- Sandpaper
- Decorative netting
- Acrylic paints in white, orange, and toffee
- Paintbrush
- Foam letter stamps
- 3 small wiggle eyes
- Hot glue

1. Paint the fan shells orange and allow to dry.

2. Stamp words on the side of the box with toffee paint and allow to dry. Tear a piece of sandpaper to fit along the bottom of the lid and glue in place. Glue assorted shells, starfish, and netting on top of the sandpaper.

3. Glue pairs of shells to form fish as shown. Paint white bubbles above the fish. Glue a wiggle eye onto each fish.

SHELLY SWITCH PLATES

Project by Linda Valentino

Create a caricature shell character for a switch plate to jazz up any room!

MATERIALS

- Assorted shells
- Wooden switch plate
- Acrylic paints in desired colors, plus white
- Paintbrush
- 1¼" (3cm) wooden circle for face
- Craft thread
- Black 22-gauge wire
- Wire cutters or old scissors
- Black permanent marker
- Foam adhesive letters
- Red chalk

1. Paint the switch plate in your desired colors and the wood circle to use as the face. Allow to dry. Add a name in foam adhesive letters.

2. Cut and shape wires for arms and legs. Position the shells, head circle, and wires. First glue down the head and the wires, then glue the shells on top.

3. Cut pieces of craft thread to form hair and glue them on. Dot on eyes and draw on a smile with black permanent marker. Color rosy cheeks with red chalk. Add a tiny dot of white paint on the cheeks. Draw stripes on a shell for a shirt.

EMBEDDED SHELL ACCESSORIES

Project by Linda Valentino

With one simple technique, you can embed a beautiful layer of shells on virtually any surface. Here are some nifty ideas to get you started.

MATERIALS (POT)

- Assorted shells
- Modeling compound such as Model Magic by Crayola
- 2½" (6.5cm)-diameter clay pot
- Blue acrylic paint
- Paintbrush
- Foam adhesive letters

1. Follow the instructions on the package to apply modeling compound to the pot. Embed shells and allow to dry.
2. Paint the pot blue and allow to dry.
3. Stick on adhesive letters.

MATERIALS (MIRROR)

- Assorted shells
- Modeling compound such as Model Magic by Crayola
- 6" (15cm) mirror with wide frame
- Ribbon for hanging (optional)
- Glue (optional)

1. Follow the instructions on the package to apply modeling compound to the mirror frame. Embed shells and allow to dry.
2. If desired, glue on a ribbon loop for hanging.

MATERIALS (BOX)

- Assorted shells
- Modeling compound such as Model Magic by Crayola
- 3¼" x 4¼" (8 x 10.5cm) storage box
- 2" x 3" (5 x 7.5cm) mirror
- Pink acrylic paint
- Paintbrush
- Hot glue

1. Follow the instructions on the package to apply modeling compound to the box top. Embed shells, leaving a space for the mirror, and allow to dry.
2. Glue the mirror to the top of the lid.
3. Paint the body of the box pink and allow to dry.

SEASIDE MONOGRAM

This monogram is a perfect gift for someone who loves the ocean. Decorate their first initial with shells so that they can have a reminder of the sea right in their home!

MATERIALS

- Assorted shells
- Wood letter
- 24" (61cm) of 1¼" (3cm)-wide brown organza ribbon
- Tacky glue

1. Apply tacky glue generously all over the surface of the letter. Cover the letter with shells and allow to dry.
2. Staple two pieces of ribbon to the back of the letter and tie a bow at the top for hanging.

SHELL BOX

Project by Julie McGuffee

This classy box takes seashell crafting to the next level. The doilies add sand-like texture, the ribbon adds a bit of glitz, and the shells simply shine.

MATERIALS

- Assorted shells
- 7" (18cm) hexagon storage box
- 6" (15cm) round tan crocheted doily
- 3" (7.5cm) tan tassel
- 24" (61cm) of tan ¼" (0.5cm)-wide satin ribbon
- 24" (61cm) of tan 1⅞" (4.5cm)-wide lace
- Tan and buttermilk acrylic paint
- Sponge brush or small sponge
- Hot glue
- Clear acrylic spray sealer

1. Paint the box with two coats of tan paint using the sponge to apply a textured pattern. Let dry.
2. Spray the box with a clear acrylic sealer and allow to dry.
3. Glue lace around the body of the box, then glue ribbon around the top edge of the lace. Glue a doily to the center of the lid. Glue a tassel in place. Glue shells on top of the doily.

ANGEL NOTECARD

If you've really enjoyed beachcombing, you probably have more shells than you can shake a stick at! Why not make a greeting card to send to a loved one and share the shells?

MATERIALS

- 1 long shell
- 3 fan shells
- 2 white felt squares, 3½" (9cm)
- 1 chipboard square, 2½" (6.5cm)
- Blue acrylic paint
- Paintbrush
- Brown chalk ink
- Glitter glue
- Hot glue

1. Paint the chipboard blue and allow to dry.
2. Ink the edges of the chipboard. Glue shells to the chipboard as shown. Glue the two pieces of felt together, then glue the chipboard to the felt.
3. Add a halo with glitter glue.

FLOWER NOTECARDS

These super flower designs made of shells look a lot more complicated than they really are. See what you can come up with using the shells you've collected!

MATERIALS

- Assorted shells
- 4" x 8" (10 x 20cm) white cardstock
- 3" x 3" (7.5 x 7.5cm) chipboard
- Green acrylic paint
- Paintbrush
- Brown chalk ink
- Twigs
- Hot glue

1. Paint the chipboard green and allow to dry.
2. Ink the edges of the chipboard. Fold the white cardstock into a 4" x 4" (10 x 10cm) card, then ink the edges.
3. Glue the chipboard to the front of the card. Glue on shells and twigs as shown.

SNAKE BLACKBOARD

Project by Linda Valentino

If you're a fan of both the beach and slithery reptiles, then this is the project for you! Create a cool snake with shells on a super useful blackboard.

MATERIALS

- 30 small assorted shells
- 5¾" x 7¾" (14.5 x 19.5cm) blackboard
- Paper towel to sponge on paint
- Acrylic paints in light, medium, and dark greens
- Foam adhesive letters
- Small piece of red foam
- 1 small wiggle eye
- Hot glue

1. Sponge all the paints together onto the blackboard border and allow to dry.
2. Adhere letters along the top.
3. Glue on shells to form a snake shape. Glue on a wiggle eye to the head of the snake. Cut out and glue on a red foam tongue.

SEASHELL SHADOW BOX

Project by Cyndi Hansen

This super shadow box is a classy way to display some of your prize seashell finds and remember a splendid trip to sunny, sandy shores.

MATERIALS

- Assorted shells
- 10" x 10" (25.5 x 25.5cm) shadow box
- Decorative scrapbook paper
- Foam adhesive letters
- Printed quote or scrapbooking items
- Black foam core board
- Hot glue
- Glue

1. Measure the inside of the box and cut three foam core pieces to fit snugly inside the box, following the diagram.

2. Cut notches in each piece of foam core, following the diagram, so the pieces will fit together inside the box. Make sure the notches are cut so the pieces fit tightly together—start small and cut larger a bit at a time. Assemble the three pieces and place them inside the box to verify the fit.

3. Remove the foam core from the box. Cut pieces of decorative paper to fit the inside of the box and glue them down as a background. If you want to use a different piece of paper in each section, put the foam core back in the box and mark the edges with a pencil so you know how big to make each piece of paper.

4. Cut strips of decorative paper to fit the edges of the pieces of foam core and glue them to the foam core. Glue the completed foam core frame inside the box.

5. Add foam adhesive letters, and glue shells and a printed quote or other scrapbooking items to the background.

6. Assemble the front of the box and add decorative strips of paper around the edges if desired.

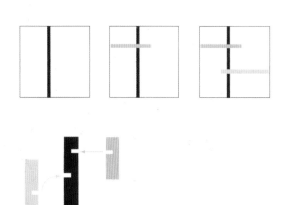

SEA

SHELL

We cannot discover new oceans until we have the courage to lose sight of the shore.

one of a kind   one of a kind

STRiNG ART SHAPES

Create attractive art while watching TV or lounging around on a rainy day. Because there are no sharp needles and only a few threads, this is also a fun project to do when traveling in the car.

MATERIALS

- Embroidery floss/craft thread
- Chipboard shapes: 3" (7.5cm) scallop edge circle, 4" (10cm) scallop edge circle, and 5" (12.5cm) snowflake
- Tape
- Glue

1. If you can't find similar chipboard shapes, simply cut out your own using sturdy cardboard.
2. To begin, tape floss to the back of the chipboard. Wrap the floss around the shapes following the photo and detailed instructions below.
3. To finish, tie a knot with the ends of the floss. Apply a dab of glue to the knot and allow to dry. Cut off the excess tails of the threads.

Large Wavy Circle

- Red floss: Tape floss to the back of the circle. Bring floss from slot #1 to slot #7, wrap around the back, and return to slot #2. Bring floss from #2 to #8 to #3 to #9. Continue around until you return to #1 again. Then begin a second round from #1 to #6. Bring thread from #2 to #7 to #3 to #8. Continue around until you return to #1 again. Tie a knot.
- Orange floss: Repeat the same pattern used for the red floss.
- Gold floss: Tape floss to the back of the circle. Wrap from #1 to #5, then around the back to #2. Bring floss from #2 to #6 to #3 to #7. Continue until you return to #1 again. Repeat a complete round. Tie a knot.

Small Wavy Circle

- Green floss: Tape floss to the back of the circle. Bring floss from slot #1 to #11, then around the back to #2. Bring floss from #2 to #12 to #3 to #13. Continue around until you return to #1 again. Tie a knot.
- Red floss: Tape floss to the back of the circle. Wrap from #1 to #13, then around the back to #2. Bring floss from #2 to #14 to #3 to #15. Continue around until you return to #1 again. Repeat two times. Tie a knot.

Snowflake

- Dark blue floss: Tape floss to the back of the snowflake. Bring floss from slot #2 to #1 on the front and to #3 in the back. Bring floss through #3 to #2 in the front, then to #4 in the back. Continue around the snowflake a total of two times. On the third round, wrap the long posts three times and the short posts one time. Tie a knot.
- Medium blue floss: Tape floss to the back of the snowflake. Continue the same wrapping pattern used for the dark blue floss for a total of four rounds. On the fifth round, wrap the long posts three times and the short posts one time. Tie a knot.
- White floss: Tape floss to the back of the snowflake. Make four complete rounds using the same pattern used for the medium blue floss. Tie a knot.
- Medium blue floss (round two): Tape thread to the back of the snowflake. Make three complete rounds using the same pattern used for the white floss. Tie a knot.

STRING ART SUN

Here comes the sun! Create depth and color with this fun project that will brighten any rainy day.

Photocopy all patterns at 200%

MATERIALS

- Embroidery floss/craft thread in red, dark orange, light orange, and gold
- 5" x 7" (12.5 x 18cm) wood board or plaque
- 28 finishing nails, 1" (2.5cm) long
- Hammer
- Glue
- Tape

1. Tape the pattern onto a wood board, and hammer in the nails as marked, being sure to leave about ½"–¼" (1.5–0.5cm) of the nail exposed.

2. Loop the floss as described below:

- Dark red (bottom layer): Tie a knot around nail #1. Wrap the floss around the nails in the following order: 13, 2, 14, 3, 15, 4, etc. Continue in this circular pattern until you reach nail #12 for the second time. Tie a knot on the final nail.

- Dark orange (second layer): Tie a knot around nail #2. Wrap the floss around the nails in the following order: 12, 3, 13, 4, 14, 5, etc. Continue in this circular pattern until you reach nail #11 for the second time. Tie a knot on the final nail.

- Light orange (third layer): Tie a knot around nail #2. Wrap the floss around the nails in the following order: 10, 3, 11, 4, 12, 5, etc. Continue in this circular pattern until you reach nail #9 for the second time. Tie a knot on the final nail.

- Gold (top layer): Tie a knot around nail #1. Wrap the floss around the nails in the following order: 7, 2, 8, 3, 9, 4, etc. Continue in this circular pattern until you reach nail #6 for the second time. Tie a knot on the final nail.

3. To finish, remove the pattern by carefully tearing it out from underneath the thread layers. Apply a dab of glue to each knot. Cut off the excess tails of floss.

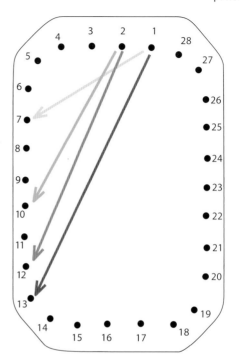

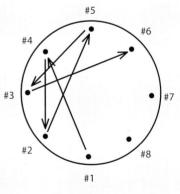

Use this basic circle wrapping sequence to practice wrapping. Tape the pattern down onto a wood board and hammer in the nails as marked, being sure to leave about ½"–¼" (1.5–0.5cm) of the nail exposed. Tie floss to nail #1. Wrap the floss around the nails in the following order: 4, 2, 5, 3, 6, 4, 7, 5, 8, 6, 1, 7, 2, 8, 3, 1. Tie a knot on the final nail.

STRING ART OWL

Hoot, hoot! This wise old owl makes a great gift. It will surely remind you of noisy summer nights full of crickets and owls calling to one another.

MATERIALS

- Embroidery floss/craft thread in burgundy, golden brown, gold, and orange
- 9" x 11½" (23 x 29cm) wood board or plaque
- 58 finishing nails, 1" (2.5cm) long
- 9" (23cm) twig
- Hammer
- Glue
- Tape

1. Tape the pattern down onto a wood board and hammer in the nails as marked, being sure to leave about ½"–¼" (1.5–0.5cm) of the nail exposed.

2. Loop the floss as described below. Note: Some threads must pass under nail #18 on the way to their destination. These are marked with a *.

- Burgundy (owl body): Tie a knot around black nail #1. Wrap the floss around the nails in the following order: 13, 2, 14, 3, 15, 4, 16, 5, 17, 6, 18, 7, 19*, 8*, 20*, 9*, 21*, 10*, 22*, 11*, 23*, 12*, 24*, 13*, 25*, 14*, 26*, 15*, 27*, 16*, 28*, 17*, 29, 18, 30, 19, 31, 20, 32, 21, 33, 22, 34, 23, 35, 24, 1, 25, 2, 26, 3, 27, 4, 28, 5, 29, 6, 30, 7, 31, 8, 32, 9, 33, 10, 34, 11, 35, 12, 1. Tie a knot on the final nail.

- Golden brown (inside the eyes): Tie a knot around red nail #1. Wrap the floss around the nails in the following order: 8, 2, 9, 3, 10, 4, 11, 5, 12, 6, 13, 7, 14, 8, 15, 9, 16, 10, 1, 11, 2, 12, 3, 13, 4, 14, 5, 15, 6, 16, 7, 1. Tie a knot on the final nail. Repeat for the other eye.

- Gold (on top of the eyes): Tie a knot around red nail #1. Wrap the floss around the nails in the following order: 7, 2, 8, 3, 9, 4, 10, 5, 11, 6, 12, 7, 13, 8, 14, 9, 15, 10, 16, 11, 1, 12, 2, 13, 3, 14, 4, 15, 5, 16, 6, 1. Tie a knot on the final nail. Repeat for the other eye.

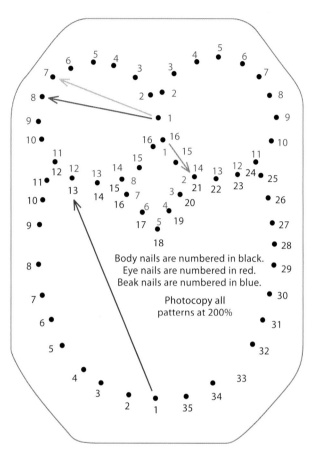

Body nails are numbered in black.
Eye nails are numbered in red.
Beak nails are numbered in blue.

Photocopy all patterns at 200%

- Orange (beak): Tie a knot around blue nail #1. Wrap the floss around the nails in the following order: 2, 1, 3, 1, 3, 1, 4, 1, 4, 1, 5, 1, 5, 1, 6, 1, 6, 1, 7, 1, 7, 1, 8, 1. Tie a knot on the final nail.

3. To finish, remove the pattern by carefully tearing it out from underneath the thread layers. Apply a dab of glue to each knot. Glue the twig in place. Cut off the excess tails of floss.

DREAM CATCHERS

Some Native American tribes believe dreams are messages sent by sacred spirits. There are many legends about dream catchers. One suggests that the web captures good dreams while bad dreams dissipate through the center hole. Another version suggests that the web traps the bad dreams to be destroyed by the morning light, allowing only good dreams to pass through the center.

MATERIALS

- Embroidery floss/craft thread
- 3" (7.5cm) or 5" (12.5cm) metal craft ring
- Size 18 needlepoint needle
- Beads or feathers
- Glue

1. Cut 4 yards (4m) of floss. Leaving an 8" (20cm) tail, tie the floss to a metal ring. Wrap the ring with floss, covering it completely, and leave another 8" (20cm) tail right next to the first one. Tie a knot snug against the ring using the two tails.

2. To make the hanging loop, simply bring the tails together and tie an overhand knot.

3. Cut 4 yards (4m) of floss. Tie one end to the ring. Then tie 12 half-hitches (or 20 if you are making the larger dream catcher) around the ring. Space them evenly with one exception: the space between the last half-hitch and the beginning knot needs to be smaller.

4. Still using the same piece of floss, tie a half-hitch in the center of the first loop created by a half-hitch from the previous step. Continue around the web, making half-hitches in the center of each loop. Keep the floss tight. Continue going around the circle and adding increasingly smaller rows of half-hitches to the previous half-hitches. When you finish in the center, secure the floss with a knot near the center of web. Place a dot of glue on the knot.

5. To finish, decorate the center with beads or a feather.

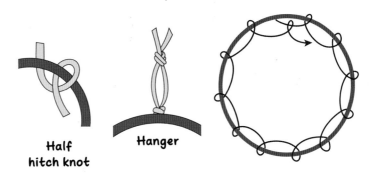

Half hitch knot

Hanger

STITCHED RAINBOW

Have a happy day and stitch a rainbow of bright colors.

MATERIALS

- Embroidery floss/craft thread in blue, green, yellow, orange, red, and purple
- 3" (7.5cm) plastic grid canvas circle
- Size 18 needlepoint needle

1. Cut a plastic canvas circle in half. Cut out the three center rows, leaving a complete set of five rows of holes.
2. Cut two of each color of floss 36" (91.5cm) long. Thread the needle with both strands of a single color. Move the needle to the center of the length, making the tails even.
3. Push the needle through the hole at the end of a row and pull the strands through, leaving a 3" (7.5cm) tail. Tie a knot with the tail to secure the ends to the canvas. Then follow the diagram to stitch the floss through the canvas. Whipstitch over the edge of the canvas on the top and bottom rows.
4. To create the fringe, cut two 4" (10cm) lengths of each color of floss. Gather and fold the strands in half. Tie a lark's head knot at the end of each row. Trim the floss ends evenly.

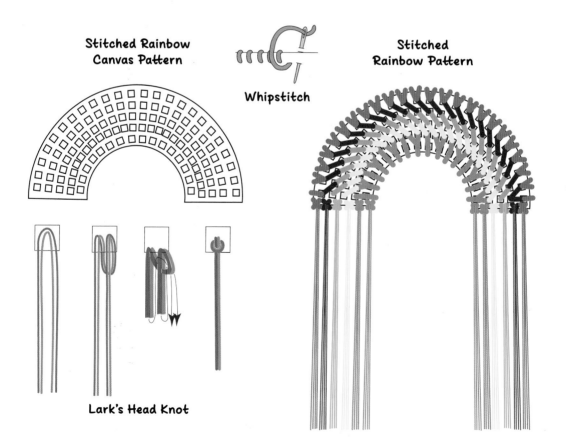

Stitched Rainbow Canvas Pattern

Whipstitch

Stitched Rainbow Pattern

Lark's Head Knot

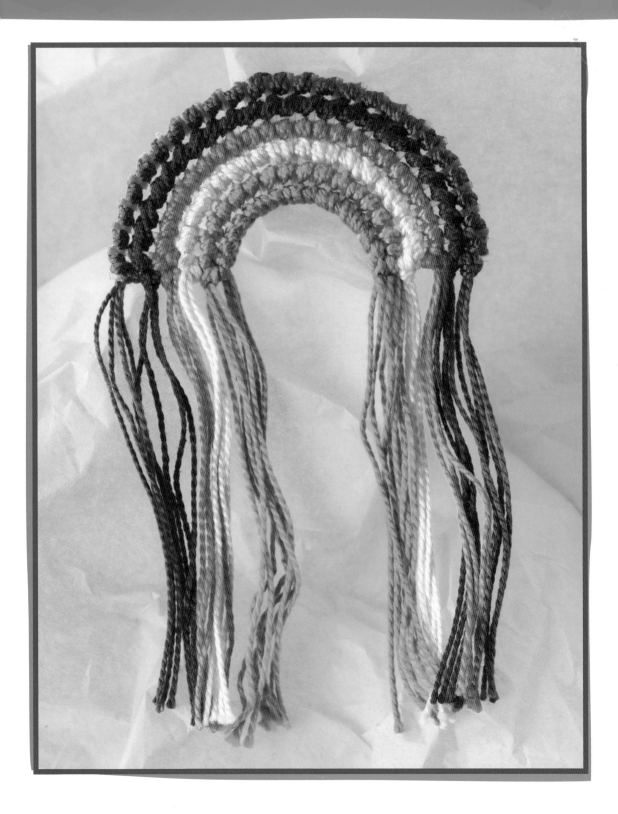

STITCHED BRACELETS

It's easy and fun to make your own bracelets. Create your own designs or use the provided patterns.

MATERIALS

- Embroidery floss/ craft thread in desired colors
- Clear plastic grid canvas
- Size 18 needlepoint needle

1. Cut a piece of canvas plastic long enough to circle your wrist and allow your hand to get through the bracelet, plus 1" (2.5cm) for the overlap. The width can be either 5 squares, 7 squares, or 11 squares, depending on the pattern you want to follow.

2. Follow a pattern to weave all the colors.

3. When you are done, overlap the two ends of the bracelet and sew a whipstitch (see page 44) around the two ends to secure the bracelet closed. You can also sew straight stitches to outline the overlap.

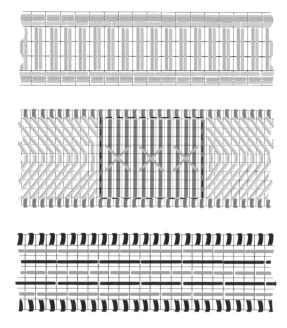

STITCHED ANIMALS

Stitched critters are easy to make. Glitter foam will give your creations extra pizzazz. Write a little note on the back and give one as a card!

MATERIALS

- Embroidery floss/craft thread
- Craft foam or glitter craft foam
- ¼" (0.5cm) and ⅛" (0.3cm) hole punches
- Size 18 needlepoint needle

1. Cut out shapes according to the patterns.
2. Punch holes with the hole punches according to the patterns. Also punch evenly-spaced holes all around the edges of the shapes (not shown on the patterns).
3. Stitch through the holes, referring to the stitch diagrams for guidance as needed.

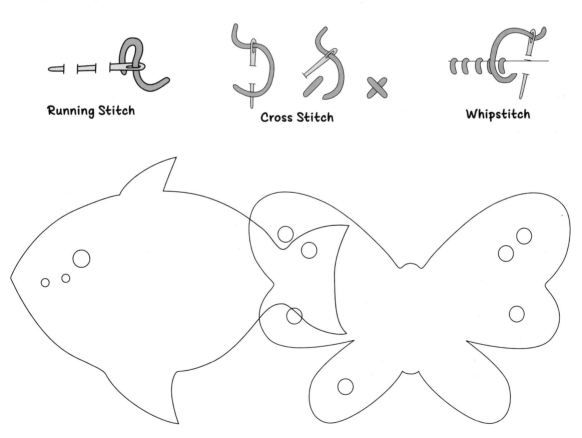

Running Stitch

Cross Stitch

Whipstitch

SPOOL NECKLACE

Every spool necklace is unique because you pick the thread combinations for each spool yourself.

MATERIALS

- Embroidery floss/craft thread
- 16 wooden ½" x ⅝" (1.5 x 1.5cm) spools
- 34 large pony beads
- Size 18 needlepoint needle
- Black acrylic paint or spray paint
- Paintbrush (if needed)
- Toggle clasp
- Glue

1. Paint the spools black. Wrap each spool with floss as desired. Glue the floss ends to the spool and allow to dry.
2. Cut four strands of black floss 24" (61cm) long. Tie all the strands to one end of the clasp. Thread all the strands into a needle.
3. String on two beads and one spool. Repeat this pattern until all the beads and spools are used.
4. Tie the other end of the clasp to the necklace.

SPOOL BRACELET

Make a bracelet that you can wear every day to match your cool spool necklace!

MATERIALS

- Embroidery floss/craft thread
- 7 wooden ½" x ⅝" (1.5 x 1.5cm) spools
- 16 large pony beads
- Size 18 needlepoint needle
- Black acrylic paint or spray paint
- Paintbrush (if needed)
- Toggle clasp
- Glue

Follow the same directions as for the Spool Necklace, but use strands that are 12" (30.5cm) long in step 2.

SPOOL KEYCHAIN

Make a fob that will help keep track of your keys or cell phone. This neat project is also a great zipper pull for your purse or backpack.

MATERIALS

- Embroidery floss/craft thread
- 4 wooden ½" x ⅝" (1.5 x 1.5cm) spools
- 10 large pony beads
- Size 18 needlepoint needle
- Black acrylic paint or spray paint
- Paintbrush (if needed)
- 1" (2.5cm) split ring
- Glue

1. Paint the spools black. Wrap each spool with floss as desired. Glue the floss ends to the spool and allow to dry.

2. Cut four strands of black floss 12" (30.5cm) long. Tie all the strands to the split ring. Assemble in the same manner as the necklace, but leave the tails untied.

3. To make the tassel, cut 16 strands of floss 4" (10cm) long. Twist the tassel threads together tightly at one end and thread through the last bead. Tie a knot. Tightly wrap the thread tails from the keychain around the tassel just below the last bead. Knot. Glue the knots to secure them and allow to dry.

FLIP-FLOPS

Step out in style all summer long with these breezy flip-flops that will keep your feet cool in more ways than one.

MATERIALS

- Embroidery floss/craft thread
- 1 pair of flip-flops
- 48 strips of colored fabric scraps,
  1" x 7" (2.5 x 18cm) each
- 2 buttons, 1¼" (3cm) diameter
- Decorative edge scissors

1. Trim the fabric strips with the decorative edge scissors. Tie fabric strips onto the flip-flop straps.

2. Tie strands of floss onto the flip-flop straps.

3. Tie a button to the center of each strap.

SUMMER SHOES

It's quick and easy to make your shoes stand out in a crowd with this technique!

MATERIALS

- Embroidery floss/craft thread
- 1 pair of colorful shoes
- 2 buttons, 1¼" (3cm) diameter

1. Cut 16 strands of floss 48" (122cm) long. Twist the strands together into a rope, then thread through the holes in the shoes in the desired pattern. Tie knots on the inside of the shoes.
2. Tie a button to the center of each shoe.

GENERAL HEMP CRAFTING TIPS

Hemp projects are typically made up of working strands, which are used to tie the knots, and center (or filler) strands, around which the knots are tied. Because of this, working strands should be five to six times as long as the desired length of the finished piece if you intend to use close, dense knots, such as square knots. The more unknotted space or beads you plan to incorporate in your design, the shorter the working strands can be. If you knot tightly, you will likely use more cord, while if you knot loosely, you won't use as much. Just keep in mind that it's always better to have too much cord than too little! You can always make smaller projects like keychains from your leftovers. For insurance, center strands should be about twice as long as the desired length of the finished piece, plus enough length to allow you to tie your ending knot easily. Again, too much is always better than too little!

To get started with any hemp project, you will typically need to measure and trim strands of hemp to the length you need, fold the strands in half to find and align the center points, and then tie an overhand knot at the folded end to form a ½" (1.5cm) loop. Before you start knotting, bring the working strands to the outside (left and right sides) of the piece.

Overhand Knot

Working Strands

Center Strands

RED BEADS BRACELET

Spice up your attire with red-hot beads.

MATERIALS

- 4 strands of hemp, 28" (71cm) long
- 6 red tile beads

Find the center of the strands. Fold and tie an overhand knot, leaving a loop. Knot adjacent pairs of strands with overhand knots, alternating a row of four knots with a row of three knots as shown in the diagram. Add beads as shown in the photo. Finish with two overhand knots, one on top of the other. Trim the ends.

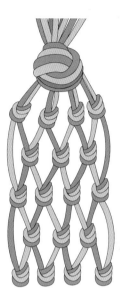

WOODEN BEADS BRACELET

A perfect pairing of organic materials, wood and hemp accent each other quite naturally!

MATERIALS

- 4 strands of hemp, 28" (71cm) long
- 9 tube beads

Find the center of the strands. Fold and tie an overhand knot, leaving a loop. Knot adjacent pairs of strands with overhand knots, alternating a row of four knots with a row of three knots as shown in the diagram for the Red Beads Bracelet. Add beads as shown in the photo. Finish with two overhand knots, one on top of the other. Trim the ends.

MULTICOLOR BEADS BRACELET

These bright primary colors are ready to match any outfit from breezy summer blouses to your favorite jeans.

MATERIALS

- 6 strands of hemp, 14" (35.5cm) long
- Assorted E beads

Tie the ends of all the cords together in an overhand knot. Skip 1" (2.5cm), then tie another overhand knot to create an opening in the bracelet that will serve as a clasp later. Spread out the six strands and start to knot adjacent pairs of strands with overhand knots, alternating a row of three knots with a row of two knots as shown in the diagram. Add beads between each row of knots as shown in the photo. Finish with two overhand knots, one on top of the other. Trim the ends.

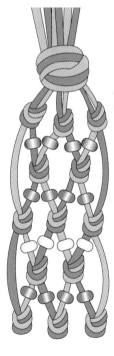

Half Knot Twist

Bring the right working strand under the center strands and over the left working strand. Bring the left working strand over the center strands and under the right working strand.

Repeat, always bringing the right strand under the center strands and over the left strand, and always bringing the left strand over the center strands and under the right strand.

Tying the half knot will naturally cause the working strands to twist around the center strands as you go, forming a spiral shape.

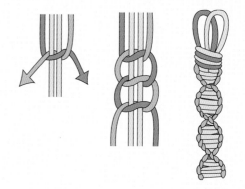

BLUE BEAD CHOKER

Surround glass beads with an intriguing spiral hemp design.

MATERIALS

- 2 strands of hemp, filler length 32" (81cm) and working length 120" (300cm)
- 1 blue lampwork bead
- 2 crystal beads

Find the center of the strands. Fold and tie an overhand knot, leaving a loop. Knot half knot twists until you reach the center of the necklace. Add the beads to the filler cord only. Continue knotting half knot twists. Finish with two overhand knots. Trim the ends.

RED BEAD CHOKER

A simply stunning combination, red and silver make a bold statement.

MATERIALS

- 2 strands of hemp, filler length 32" (81cm) and working length 120" (300cm)
- 1 red tube bead
- 2 silver tube beads

Find the center of the strands. Fold and tie an overhand knot, leaving a loop. Knot half knot twists until you reach the center of the necklace. Add the beads to all the strands. Continue knotting half knot twists. Finish with two overhand knots. Trim the ends.

BONE AND BRASS CHOKER

Project by Edith Snyder

Delicate knotwork combines quietly with the earthy textures of brass and bone. The understated artistry gives this choker universal appeal.

MATERIALS

- 2 strands of hemp, filler length 30" (76cm) and working length 60" (153cm)
- 11 black bone beads
- 22 brass beads

Find the center of the strands. Fold and tie an overhand knot, leaving a loop. Knot half knot twists, adding beads to one filler cord only as you go, running the other filler cord behind the beads. Finish with two overhand knots. Trim the ends.

You can make any choker into a necklace just by making the strands of hemp longer!

Square Knot

Bring the right working strand under the center strands and over the left working strand. Bring the left working strand over the center strands and under the right working strand.

Bring the right working strand over the center strands and under the left working strand. Bring the left working strand under the center strands and over the right working strand.

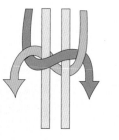
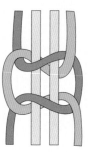

SILVER BEAD CHOKER

Solid silver creates a very cool effect on this choker.

MATERIALS

- 2 strands of hemp, filler length 36" (91.5cm) and working length 60" (153cm)
- 15 silver beads

Find the center of the strands. Fold and tie an overhand knot, leaving a loop. Tie four square knots. Add a bead to all the strands. Tie two square knots, then add another bead. Continue like this, tying two square knots between each bead, until you reach the end and finish with four square knots. Finish with two overhand knots. Trim the ends.

MULTICOLOR CHOKER

Square knots between each bead make the beads all face the same direction. Check out the adjustable closure, too. It's a technique you could apply to any necklace.

MATERIALS

- 2 strands of hemp, filler length 18" (45.5cm) and working length 60" (153cm)
- Assorted beads

Find the center of the strands. Fold and tie an overhand knot, leaving a loop. Tie three more overhand knots at ½" (1.5cm) intervals to make an adjustable closure. Tie half knot twists (see page 54) for 3½" (9cm). Then start adding beads, tying a square knot between each bead. When you are done with the beads, tie half knot twists for another 3½" (9cm). Add one large bead to work as a closure bead and finish with one overhand knot. Trim the ends.

BLUE BEAD CHOKER

This delicate knotwork design creates an attractive, thin line that is well suited to displaying focal beads.

MATERIALS

- 2 strands of hemp, filler length 18" (45.5cm) and working length 120" (300cm)
- 3 blue clay beads
- 2 small black beads

Find the center of the strands. Fold and tie an overhand knot, leaving a loop. Tie square knots for 4½" (11.5cm). Add the beads, tying one square knot between each bead. Tie square knots for another 4½" (11.5cm). Finish with two overhand knots. Trim the ends.

OLIVE WOOD BEAD BRACELET

Smooth wood beads make this bracelet a joy to wear.

MATERIALS

- 2 strands of hemp, filler length 24" (61cm) and working length 55" (140cm)
- 13 wood beads

Find the center of the strands. Fold and tie an overhand knot, leaving a loop. Tie a square knot (see page 56). Add a bead to the filler strands. Repeat this pattern to the end of the bracelet, then tie one more square knot. Finish with an overhand knot. Trim the ends.

BiG BEAD BRACELET

Create a unique look by alternating bead sizes and styles. This combination of chunky colors and silver is a real eye-catcher.

MATERIALS

- 2 strands of hemp, filler length 24" (61cm) and working length 68" (173cm)
- 3 large clay beads
- 4 small silver beads

Find the center of the strands. Fold and tie an overhand knot, leaving a loop. Tie square knots (see page 56) for 2" (5cm). Add beads to the filler strands, tying one square knot between each bead. After adding all the beads, tie square knots for 2" (5cm). Finish with an overhand knot. Trim the ends.

Turquoise and Silver Bracelet

GOLD BEAD BRACELET

Small gold beads give this bracelet a subtle shine.

MATERIALS

- 2 strands of hemp, filler length 24" (61cm) and working length 68" (173cm)
- 5 gold beads

Find the center of the strands. Fold and tie an overhand knot, leaving a loop. Tie square knots (see page 56) for 2" (5cm). Add beads to the filler strands, tying two square knots between each bead. After adding all the beads, tie square knots for 2" (5cm). Finish with an overhand knot. Trim the ends.

TURQUOISE AND SILVER BRACELET

Combine turquoise and silver for a traditional Southwest style.

MATERIALS

- 2 strands of hemp, filler length 24" (61cm) and working length 68" (173cm)
- 3 blue tube beads
- 4 silver tube beads

Find the center of the strands. Fold and tie an overhand knot, leaving a loop. Tie square knots (see page 56) for 2" (5cm). Add beads to the filler strands, tying two square knots between each bead. After adding all the beads, tie square knots for 2" (5cm). Finish with an overhand knot. Trim the ends.

MULTICOLOR DISK BEAD BRACELET

These beads are too much fun! The dots on the outsides of the disks look like eyes.

MATERIALS

- 2 strands of hemp, filler length 24" (61cm) and working length 68" (173cm)
- 26 glass disk beads

Find the center of the strands. Fold and tie an overhand knot, leaving a loop. Tie two square knots (see page 56). Add a bead to each working cord. Tie two more square knots. Repeat this pattern for the length of the bracelet. After adding all the beads, tie two square knots. Finish with an overhand knot. Trim the ends.

RED BEAD CHOKER

Surround your neck with the fiery brilliance of ruby red sparkle.

MATERIALS

- 2 strands of hemp, filler length 24" (61cm) and working length 68" (173cm)
- Red E beads

Find the center of the strands. Fold and tie an overhand knot, leaving a loop. Tie one square knot (see page 56) to get started. Add a bead to each working strand. Tie one square knot. Repeat adding beads and tying square knots for the length of the choker. Finish with an overhand knot. Trim the ends.

SHELL CHOKER

This is a unisex, beachy look that never goes out of style.

MATERIALS

- 2 strands of hemp, filler length 24" (61cm) and working length 90" (229cm)
- 64 white shell chip beads
- Silver clasp with extender chain

Find the center of the strands. Fold and tie an overhand knot, leaving a loop. Tie square knots (see page 56) for 1" (2.5cm). Add two shell chips to the filler strands. Tie one square knot. Repeat this pattern for the length of the choker. Tie square knots for another 1" (2.5cm). Finish with an overhand knot. Trim the ends.

BALL CHAIN NECKLACE

Ball chain provides the silver in this versatile, popular hemp necklace accessory.

MATERIALS

- 1 strand of hemp, 98" (249cm)
- 18" (45.5cm) of silver 4mm ball chain
- Glue

Fold the hemp strand in half. Tuck one end of the ball chain into the fold. Tie a square knot (see page 56) around the ball. Then tie one square knot between each ball for the length of the chain. Glue the last knot securely. Trim the ends.

HEMP BEAD BUDDIES

These charming little fellows are a cinch to make and don't require any complicated knots! Use different beads to create a variety of sizes and shapes of bead buddies, then trade them with friends!

MATERIALS FOR LARGE BEAD BUDDIES

- 14" (35.5cm) strand of hemp for head/ body/legs
- 7" (18cm) strand of hemp for arms
- Large bead for body
- Medium bead for head
- 2 to 12 small beads for arms and legs

MATERIALS FOR MEDIUM BEAD BUDDIES

- 12" (30.5cm) strand of hemp for head/ body/legs
- 6" (15cm) strand of hemp for arms
- Medium bead for body
- Small bead for head
- 2 to 12 small beads for arms and legs

MATERIALS FOR SMALL BEAD BUDDIES

- 10" (25.5cm) strand of hemp for head/ body/legs
- 5" (12.5cm) strand of hemp for arms
- Medium bead for body
- Small bead for head
- 2 to 12 tiny beads for arms and legs

1. Find the center of the head/body/legs strand. Fold and tie an overhand knot, leaving a loop.
2. Add a head bead and body bead to the strands. Do not push them together. Then separate the two strands and add leg beads to each strand. Tie off loosely.
3. Thread the arms strand through the body strands between the two beads. Add arm beads to both ends of the arms strand, then tie both ends off tightly.
4. Tighten the leg knots and cut off excess cord.

HEMP WIND CHIME

This nifty DIY wind chime is light enough to catch a breeze and cool enough to catch everyone's eye!

MATERIALS

- 6 strands of hemp, 66" (168cm) long
- 2 bone 3-hole spacer bars
- 3 brown 1¾" (4.5cm) beads
- 6 small brass beads
- 6 small brass bells with loops at top

1. Find the center of the strands. Fold and tie an overhand knot, leaving a 1" (2.5cm) loop for hanging. Separate the strands into three groups of four. Tie half knot twists (see page 54) for 1½" (4cm) with each group.

2. Thread each group of strands through a hole in a spacer bar. Add one brass bead, one brown bead, and one brass bead to each group of strands. Thread each group of strands through a hole in a second spacer bar.

3. Tie half knot twists for 1" (2.5cm) with each group. Then tie an overhand knot with each group.

4. Add a bell to one pair of strands from a group, positioning the bell about 4" (10cm) down the strand. Fold the strands up and tie an overhand knot, leaving a small loop at the end with the bell hanging freely in the loop. Pull the knot snug and trim the ends. Repeat with the rest of the pairs of strands, hanging the bells at slightly different heights.

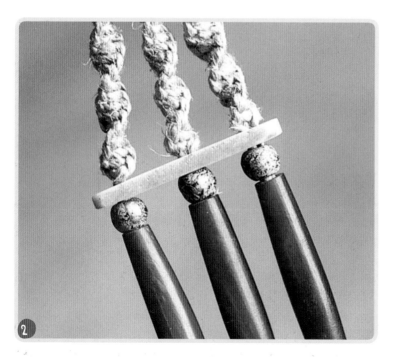

HEMP WATCH BAND

With this technique, you can make a custom watch band for any suitable watch! Make one for your dad, a friend, or yourself. You can always make another in new colors if you are ready for a change!

MATERIALS

- 4 strands of hemp, 72" (183cm) long
- 3 strands of hemp, 6" (15cm) long
- 4 small blue beads
- 1 watch face with bars
- 1 watch buckle

1. Fold the four long strands in half and attach them to the watch buckle using lark's head knots, placing two on each side of the buckle tongue. Using the two outside strands from each side as one "strand," tie ten square knots (see page 56) over the four center strands.

2. Separate the strands into two groups of four. Tie one square knot with each group. Using the three outside strands from each group, tie six half knot twists (see page 54) with each group. Add a bead to the two inside strands not used in the half knot twists.

3. Repeat step 2.

4. Separate the strands into two groups of four. Tie one square knot with each group. Thread the strands down between the bar and watch face, under the watch face, and out up between the watch face and bar on the other side. Repeat step 2 twice. Then separate the strands into two groups of four and tie one square knot with each group.

5. Using the two outside strands from each group as one "strand," tie two square knots over the four center strands. Trim two of the center strands and dot the cut ends with glue. Tie eight square knots over the two remaining center strands. (To make the band longer, add more square knots; to make it shorter, tie fewer square knots.) Pull the last knot very tight.

6. Separate the remaining strands into three groups of two. Braid the strands for 1½" (4cm). Fold the braid to the back side of the band and glue in place. Before the glue is dry, make holes for the buckle tongue by pushing the end of a large needle through the band between each square knot. Trim the ends when the glue is dry.

7. To create a band strap, braid the three short strands for 1½" (4cm). Circle this braid around the band about 1" (2.5cm) from the buckle. Secure the ends to the back side of the band with glue. Trim the ends when the glue is dry.

Lark's Head Knot

Basic Three-Strand Braid

friendship Bracelets

GENERAL FRIENDSHIP BRACELET CRAFTING TIPS

Review the instructions and knots on these pages to learn all the techniques you'll need to make any of the friendship bracelets in this section! Unless otherwise stated, use 36" (91.5cm) strands of embroidery floss for each color in a design. For designs with two strands of the same color, use 72" (183cm) strands doubled over unless otherwise stated.

Starting any bracelet

Tie the strands for your bracelet together using an overhand knot with a ½" (1.5cm) loop at the top. For bracelets using 36" (91.5cm) strands, double over the first few inches to form the loop. For bracelets using 72" (183cm) strands, fold the strands in half to form the loop. Secure the knotted end of your bracelet to your workspace with tape.

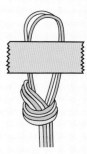

Basic forward knot

Bring the leftmost strand over and then under the strand immediately to the right of it. Pull the end of the working strand through the loop that has formed. Pull the knot up firmly against the overhand knot at the end of the bracelet. This is called a half hitch knot.

   Repeat, tying a second half hitch knot using the same strand. Pull the second knot up firmly against the first. You will see that the strands switch places. Always tie two half hitches for each knot before moving on to the next strand.

Basic backward knot

A backward knot is the reverse of a forward knot and is tied onto the strand to the left to move the knot backward. Follow the illustrations to tie a backward knot. Remember, always tie two half hitches for each knot before moving on to the next strand.

Forward-backward knot

Tie a forward knot with the leftmost strand. This moves the strand to the right. Then, using the same strand, tie a backward knot. This moves the strand back where it started.

Backward-forward knot

Tie a backward knot with the rightmost strand. This moves the strand to the left. Then, using the same strand, tie a forward knot. This moves the strand back where it started.

To end

Depending on the number of threads your bracelet uses and your desired look, there are several ways you can finish your bracelet.

Option 1: Divide the strands at the end of the bracelet into three groups and braid them together. Secure with an overhand knot and trim.

Option 2: Divide the strands at the end of the bracelet into six groups. Braid the three left groups together and the three right groups together. Secure with overhand knots and trim.

Option 3: Tie all the strands at the end of the bracelet together in an overhand knot. Use the loose ends to tie the bracelet onto your wrist.

STRiPED FRIENDSHiP BRACELETS

This traditional design makes a smooth-to-the-touch, flat bracelet that is simply classy.

1. For bracelets with an even number of strands, start with 72" (183cm) strands doubled over. For bracelets with an odd number of strands, start with 36" (91.5cm) single strands. Tie the strands together using an overhand knot with a ½" (1.5cm) loop at the top. Arrange the strands to create the pattern you desire, using the illustrations shown here for reference. Note how the placement of your strands will affect where the stripes appear in the finished bracelet.

2. Tie rows of forward or backward knots across the strands one at a time until you reach the desired length. Remember, always tie the half hitch twice for each forward or backward knot before moving on to the next strand. You will always tie one fewer knot than the total number of strands in your design. If you are using eight strands, you will tie seven knots across the bracelet. For four strands, you will tie three knots.

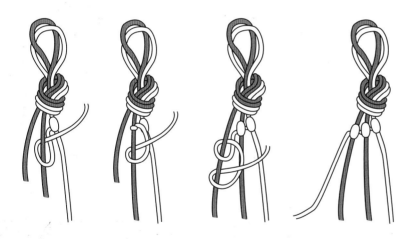

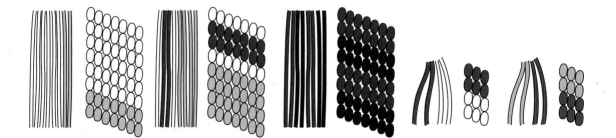

CHEVRON FRIENDSHIP BRACELETS

Chevrons are so in right now. They are super modern, super colorful, and super cool. Choose colors that mean something to you.

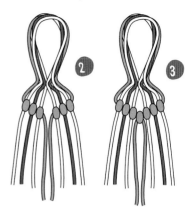

1. Start with four 72" (183cm) strands doubled over for eight strands total. Tie the strands together using an overhand knot with a ½" (1.5cm) loop at the top. Arrange the strands so the colors form a symmetrical pattern, using the illustrations below for reference. For a thicker bracelet, use more strands.

2. Using the outer left strand, tie three forward knots working toward the center of the bracelet. Then, using the outer right strand, tie three backward knots working toward the center of the bracelet.

3. Tie a forward or backward knot at the center of the bracelet with the two center strands. Repeat steps 2–3 for each row until you reach the desired length.

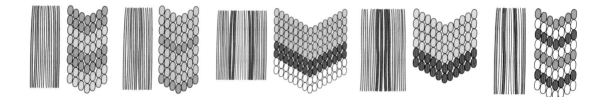

ZiG-ZAG FRIENDSHIP BRACELETS

Feeling quirky? Why not try this zig-zag design? You're sure to have people wondering just how you achieved the unique shape of this bracelet. Surprise—it's really quite easy!

1. Start with four 72" (183cm) strands doubled over for eight strands total. Tie the strands together using an overhand knot with a ½" (1.5cm) loop at the top. Arrange the strands so the colors form a symmetrical pattern. To create a two-tone bracelet, place four strands of one color on the left side, and four strands of another color on the right side, as shown in the illustration.

2. To begin, tie four rows of backward knots across the bracelet using the four right strands. You will see the rows begin to slant to the left.

3. Tie four rows of forward knots across the bracelet using the four left strands. You will see the rows slant to the right.

4. Tie four additional rows of forward knots across the bracelet using the four left strands. This will give you a total of eight rows that slant to the right.

5. Tie eight rows of backward knots across the bracelet. Then, tie eight rows of forward knots. Repeat until you reach the desired length.

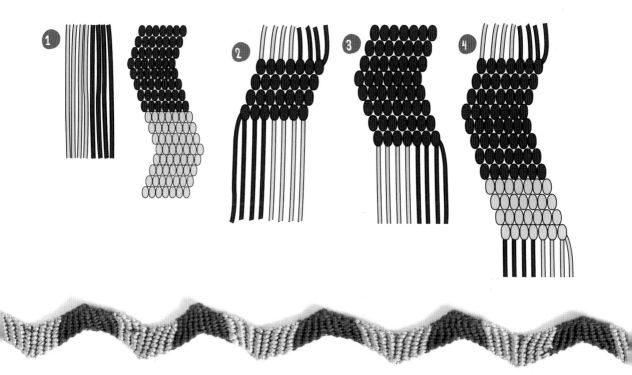

SINGLE WAVE FRIENDSHIP BRACELETS

Create a smooth single wave bracelet with or without beads if you're feeling like you just want to go with the flow.

1. Start with ten 36" (91.5cm) single strands. Tie the strands together using an overhand knot with a ½" (1.5cm) loop at the top. Position the strand colors as shown in the illustration. Note that the two outer strands on the left side are the base strands on which all your knots will be tied.

2. Using the strand that is third from the left, tie a backward knot on the base strand immediately to the left of it. Tie another backward knot on the outer base strand. Repeat, tying each of the remaining seven strands onto the base strands using backward knots. Make the last knot you tie a backward-forward knot.

3. To reverse the direction of the wave, use the bottom working strand to tie a forward knot on the outer right base strand only. Use each of the remaining strands to tie a forward knot on each of the base strands. Make the last knot you tie a forward-backward knot. Repeat steps 2–3 until you reach the desired length.

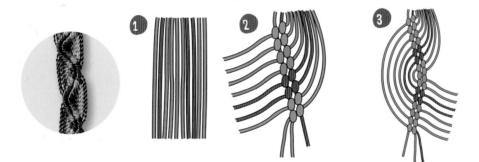

DOUBLE WAVE FRIENDSHIP BRACELETS

Create a vibrant double wave bracelet if you are in the mood for funky patterns and contrasting spots of color!

1. Start with six 72" (183cm) strands doubled over for twelve strands total. Tie the strands together using an overhand knot with a ½" (1.5cm) loop at the top. Arrange the strands so the colors form a symmetrical pattern, using the illustration for reference.

2. To begin, use the outer strands to tie knots working from each side of the bracelet toward the center. Tie five knots on each side for the first row, four knots on each side for the second row, then three knots, and then two.

3. Starting with the third strand from the left, tie two backward knots working toward the outside of the bracelet. Repeat with the remaining three strands on the left side. Do the same on the right side of the bracelet, tying two forward knots for four rows on the right side.

4. Tie a forward or backward knot with the two center strands. Using the right center strand, tie a forward-backward knot on the strand immediately to the right of it.

5. Using the left center strand, tie a backward-forward knot on the strand immediately to the left of it.

6. Tie a forward or backward knot with the two center strands.

7. Starting with the fourth strand from the left, tie two forward knots, working toward the center of the bracelet. Repeat with the remaining three strands on the left side. Do the same on the right side of the bracelet, tying two backward knots for four rows on the right side.

8. Repeat steps 3—7 until you reach the desired length.

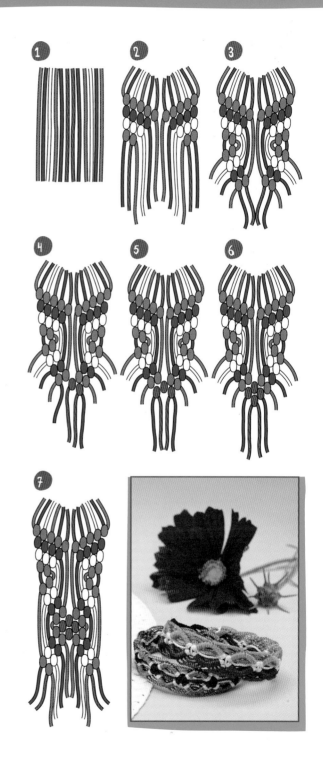

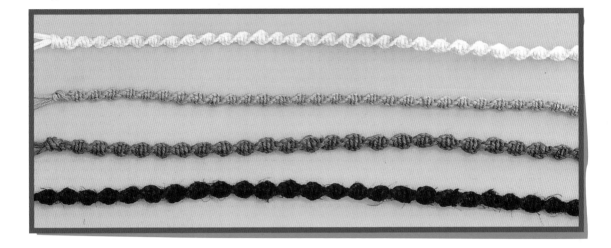

HALF KNOT TWIST FRIENDSHIP BRACELETS

This is a great project if you want to stick with solid colors and create a bracelet pretty quickly. Make lots of them for all your friends!

1. This knot is called a half knot because it is the first half of a square knot. Start with two 72" (183cm) strands doubled over for four strands total.

2. Tie the strands together using an overhand knot with a ½" (1.5cm) loop at the top.

3. Bring the outer right strand under the center strands and over the outer left strand. Bring the outer left strand over the center strands and under the outer right strand.

4. Repeat step 3 until you reach the desired length. The outer right strand will always go under the center strands and over the outer left strand. The outer left strand will always go over the center strands and under the outer right strand.

5. Tying a half knot will naturally cause the outer strands to twist around the center strands as you work, forming a spiral shape. Note that if you use two different colors for the outer strands, the colors at the center and the outside edges of the bracelet will alternate with every knot.

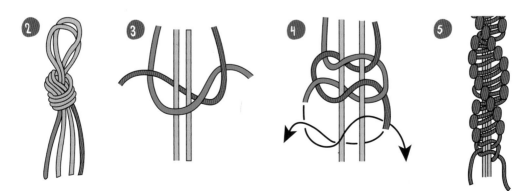

Adding Beads

To add beads to the center of the bracelet, thread them onto one or both center strands and tie half knots around them with the outer strands. To add beads to the outside edges of the bracelet, thread them onto one or both outer strands.

Adding Daisies

To create each daisy, thread one seed bead on the center strands and three seed beads on each of the outer strands.

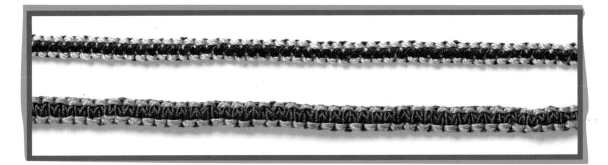

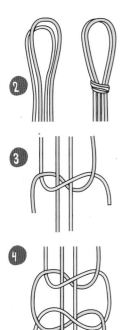

SQUARE KNOTS FRIENDSHIP BRACELETS

The square knot is a pretty simple knot that is easy to get the hang of, and it's great for incorporating beads.

1. Start with two 72" (183cm) strands doubled over for four strands total.

2. Arrange the strands to create the pattern you desire. To create a dual-color bracelet, make sure the outermost strands are two different colors. Tie the strands together using an overhand knot with a ½" (1.5cm) loop at the top.

3. Bring the outer right strand under the center strands and over the outer left strand. Bring the outer left strand over the center strands and under the outer right strand.

4. To finish the square knot, bring the outer right strand over the center strands and under the outer left strand. Bring the outer left strand under the center strands and over the outer right strand. Repeat steps 3—4 until you reach the desired length.

Adding Beads

Add small beads like seed beads to the outer working strands as you tie your square knots. You can also add beads to one or both of the center strands as you work.

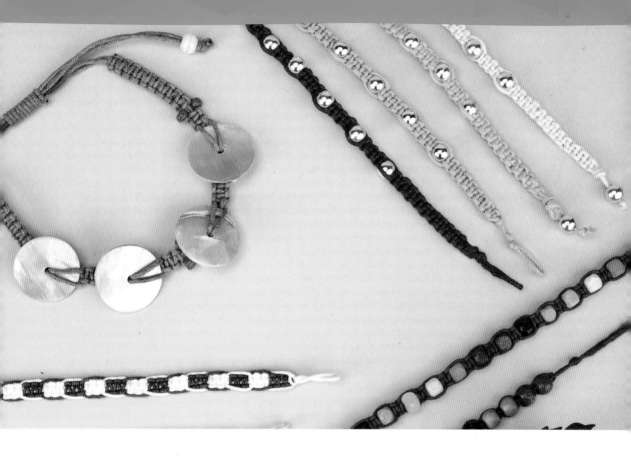

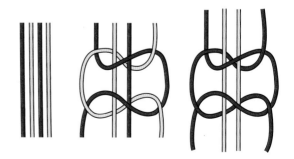

Alternating Colors

To alternate colors, use two strands of the same color for the outer strands and two strands of the same color for the inner strands. Work several square knots with the outer strands. To switch colors, bring the inner strands to the outside and work several square knots with them.

To create a dual-color alternating bracelet, arrange the strands so the colors alternate. Tie several square knots with the outer strands. To switch colors, bring two strands of the same color to the outside and work several square knots with them.

SMALL DIAMONDS FRIENDSHIP BRACELETS

These delicate diamonds are just the ticket if you prefer pretty but detailed designs.

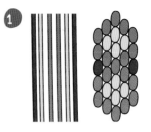

1. Start with three 72" (183cm) strands doubled over for six strands total. Tie the strands together using an overhand knot with a ½" (1.5cm) loop at the top. Arrange the strands so the colors form a symmetrical pattern, using the illustration for reference.

2. Tie a forward or backward knot with the two center strands.

3. Using the right center strand, tie two forward knots working toward the outside of the bracelet.

4. Using the left center strand, tie two backward knots working toward the outside of the bracelet.

5. Tie a forward or backward knot with the two center strands.

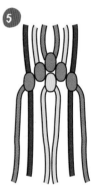

6. Using the right center strand, tie a forward-backward knot on the strand immediately to the right of it.

7. Using the left center strand, tie a backward-forward knot on the strand immediately to the left of it.

8. Tie a forward or backward knot with the two center strands.

9. Using the outer left strand, tie two forward knots working toward the center of the bracelet. Do the same with the outer right strand, tying two backward knots working toward the center. Tie a forward or backward knot with the two center strands.

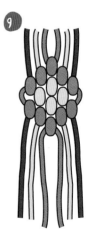

10. Using the outer left strand, tie a forward-backward knot on the strand immediately to the right of it. Do the same with the outer right strand, tying a backward-forward knot on the strand immediately to the left of it. Repeat from step 3 until you reach the desired length.

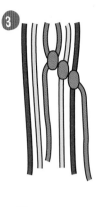

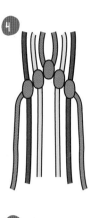

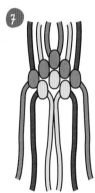

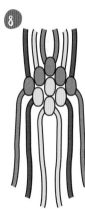

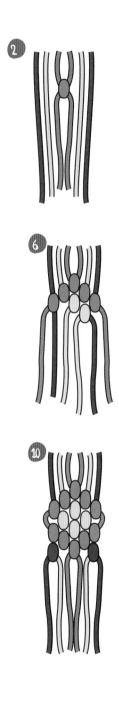

WiDE DiAMONDS FRiENDSHiP BRACELETS

The wide diamond pattern offers one of the most gorgeous combinations of colors you can find in a friendship bracelet. It's worth the extra effort!

1. Start with six 72" (183cm) strands doubled over for twelve strands total. Tie the strands together using an overhand knot with a ½" (1.5cm) loop at the top. Arrange the strands so the colors form a symmetrical pattern, using the illustration for reference.

2. Using the outer left strand, tie five forward knots working toward the center of the bracelet. Do the same with the outer right strand, tying five backward knots working toward the center. Tie a forward or backward knot with the two center strands. Repeat this pattern for the next four rows.

3. Using the outer left strand, tie three forward knots and one forward-backward knot working toward the center of the bracelet. Do the same with the outer right strand, tying three backward knots and one backward-forward knot working toward the center.

4. Repeat the pattern from step 3 to tie two knots from each side on the next row. Make the second knot on the left side a forward-backward knot and the second knot on the right side a backward-forward knot.

5. Using the second strand from the left side, tie a backward knot on the outer left strand. Do the same with the second strand from the right, tying a forward knot on the outer right strand.

6. Using the fourth strand from the left side, tie a row of backward knots, working toward the outside of the bracelet. Do the same with the fourth strand from the right side, tying a row of forward knots working toward the outside.

7. Repeat the pattern from step 6 using the left and right center strands, but make the last knot on the left side a backward-forward knot and the last knot on the right side a forward-backward knot.

8. Tie a forward or backward knot with the center strands. Then, use the right center strand to tie two forward knots and one forward-backward knot working toward the outside. Do the same with the left center strand, tying two backward knots and one backward-forward knot working toward the outside.

9. Tie a forward or backward knot with the center strands. Use the right center strand to tie a forward-backward knot on the strand immediately to the right of it. Use the left center strand to tie a backward-forward knot on the strand immediately to the left of it. Tie a forward or backward knot with the center strands.

10. Using the fourth strand from the left, tie two forward knots working toward the center of the bracelet. Do the same with the fourth strand from the right, tying two backward knots working toward the center. Tie a forward or backward knot with the center strands. Repeat the pattern using the second strand from the left and right side, tying four knots for each side, and then knotting the center strands.

11. Repeat steps 3–10 until you reach the desired length. To change colors, repeat step 2, but only work four rows instead of five.

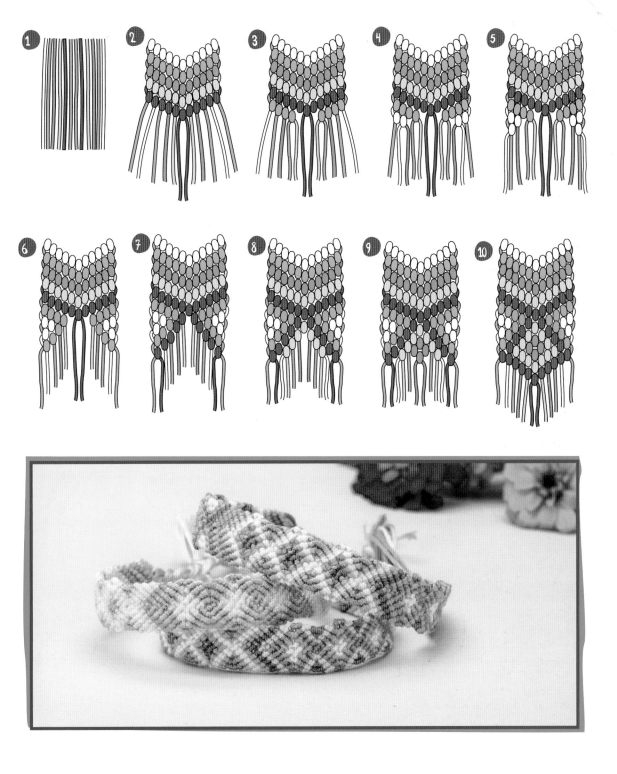

FRIENDSHIP BRACELET CRAFTS

Your friendship bracelets don't have to just stay bracelets! There are many ways you can incorporate them into accessories and make them useful as well as stylish. Take a look at the ideas on these pages to get inspired!

Headband

Glue a finished bracelet onto the center of a plain, flat headband.

Coin Purse

Fold back the knot at the beginning of a very wide bracelet (such as a Wide Diamonds Friendship Bracelet from page 82, but done with 48 strands instead of 12 strands). Fold the bracelet again 2½" (6.5cm) from the first fold. Sew the sides of the folded sides together. Fold the end flap over to close the purse.

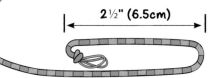

2½" (6.5cm)

Key Chain

Fold a bracelet in half over a key ring. Sew the sides together.

Barrette

Fold a bracelet in half, then glue it onto the top of a metal barrette.

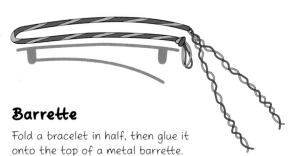

BASIC LANYARD

Here you will learn how to make the simplest kind of 4-strand plastic lace lanyard in two different styles of stitches.

MATERIALS

- 2 strands of plastic lace, at least 24" (61cm) long for a short finished piece
- Lanyard hook or key ring
- Tape

Getting Started

1. Thread two strands of plastic lace through a lanyard hook until the hook is at the middle of the laces. Fasten down with a piece of tape for the first stitch; remove the tape after step 5.
2. Fold one end back.
3. Fold the next end over it.
4. Fold the third end over the second.
5. Fold the fourth end over the third and under the loop formed by the first fold.
6. Remove the tape, and pull the stitch tight.

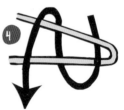

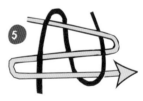

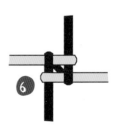

Helpful Photos

1. Here you can see the first stitch with the lace still taped down (step 5).
2. A regular square stitch will look like this before you tighten it (step 10a).
3. When finishing a project, you will thread each strand up through the square formed by the loose final stitch (step 12).
4. Your finished lanyard will look something like this.

The Square Stitch

7A. To make a square stitch, fold the first strand over itself.

8A. Fold the other laces one at a time, starting here with the second lace.

9A. Fold the third lace.

10A. Fold the fourth lace, making sure to thread it under the loop formed by the first lace.

11A. Tighten. As you continue making square stitches, the box pattern will appear.

The Round Stitch

7B. To make a round stitch, fold the first strand over the opposite one, at an angle.

8B. Fold the adjacent strand over it, again at an angle.

9B. Fold the third strand.

10B. Fold the fourth strand, making sure to thread it through the loop of the first strand.

11B. Tighten; the stitch is rotated from the first. Make the second and succeeding stitches the same as the first—if it went clockwise, continue clockwise; if it went counterclockwise, continue counterclockwise. As you continue making round stitches, the spiral pattern will appear.

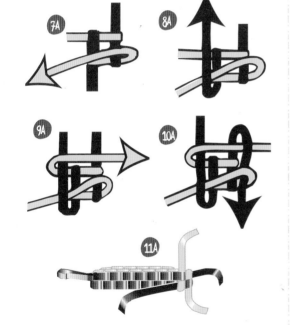

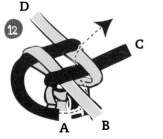

Finishing

12. To finish your project, make a final square stitch, and leave it loose. Run strand A under strand B and up through the center. Run strand B under C and up the center. Continue with C and D, so all ends are together in the center. Now pull tight, and trim off the ends at the desired length.

BEADED AND BUTTON ZiPPER PULLS

It's quite simple to add a variety of beads to a stitched zipper pull. You can create many different designs, too. Adding beads and buttons instantly makes a plastic lace craft into something unique and you!

MATERIALS

- 2 strands of plastic lace, at least 24" (61cm)
- Lanyard hook or key ring
- Pony beads, heart beads, or buttons
- Tape

Basic Beaded Zipper Pulls

1. Start off with nine square stitches, and then thread all four ends through a pony bead. When they emerge from the pony bead, spread the ends out so that two of the same color are opposite each other.

2. Proceed to make a new square stitch. After five square stitches, thread the four ends through a second pony bead. Make five or six more square stitches. You may finish in the usual way, or run the four strands through a third pony bead, then run two strands through a second time.

Kissing Hearts Zipper Pull

Start with nine round stitches. Thread all four ends through one heart bead, top first, then through a second heart bead, bottom first. After they emerge from the second bead, make nine more round stitches and finish.

Caged Bead Zipper Pull

Start with four round or square stitches. Pull them very tight. Make two more stitches, and leave them loose. Take a pony bead, insert it into the cage of the first stitch, and tighten the cage around it by pulling tight the second stitch. Make four more very tight stitches. Again make two loose stitches, insert a pony bead inside the first one, and tighten the second one around it. Repeat the process once or twice, so that you have three or four caged pony beads. After four additional stitches, finish and trim.

Button Zipper Pulls

If you are using buttons, consider the button loop size. Buttons come with small loops, large loops, or holes in them. If they come with small loops, like the dinosaur and flowers zipper pulls, just run a strand through the loop wherever you want the button placed, and continue stitching. If there is a large loop, run all four strands through it, and pick up the stitch on the far side, as with the pony bead zipper pulls. If there are holes in the bead, run one or two strands through, and continue stitching.

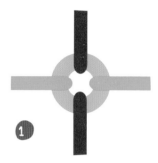

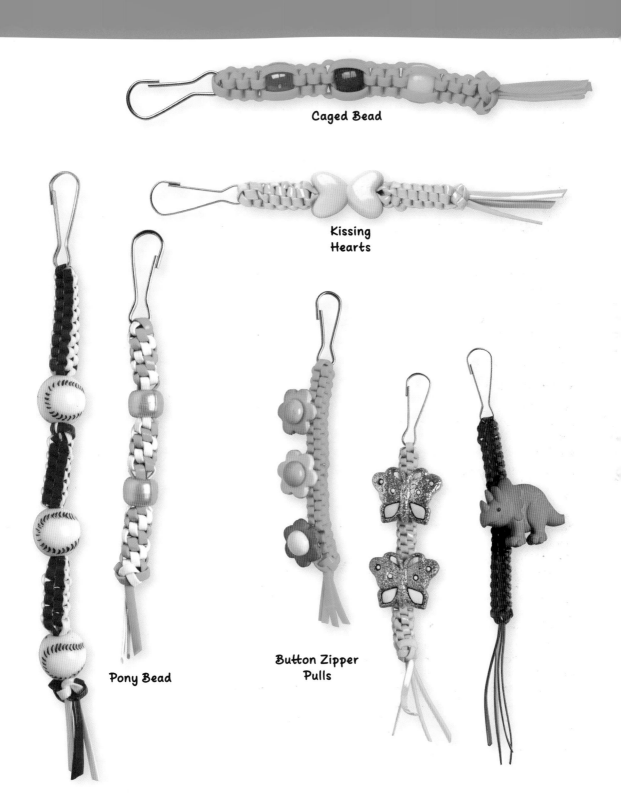

Caged Bead

Kissing
Hearts

Pony Bead

Button Zipper
Pulls

ZiPPER BRAiD BRACELET

This zipper effect is edgy and stylish. It's also super easy and fast, so don't hesitate to make a whole set!

MATERIALS

- 24" (61cm) plastic lace in color A (the center color)
- 48" (122cm) plastic lace in color B (the weaving color)
- Lanyard hook or paper clip
- Tape or safety pin

1. The short lace will be lace A and the long lace will be lace B. Fold lace A in half and stack the laces together.

2. Tie an overhand knot ½" (1.5cm) from the fold. Attach a lanyard hook or paper clip to the fold.

3. Tape or pin the hook to a surface, such as the table or the leg of your jeans, to make it easier to braid. Hold the A strands straight down and keep the B strand flat against them as you weave. Bring B between the two A strands down under A2, back up and over A2, and between the A strands down under A1 until it is back on the left side where it started.

4. Slide the stitches up and together snugly as you weave. Continue repeating the step 3 weaving pattern until the bracelet fits your wrist.

5. Remove the tape and hook from the loop end of the bracelet. Tie two overhand knots, one on top of the other, with the ends of the lace. Trim the tails.

6. Wrap the bracelet around your wrist and slide the knot into the loop for the closure.

To make a keychain, you will need 12" (30.5cm) of color A and 24" (61cm) of color B. Make the braid shorter and leave the lanyard hook in place.

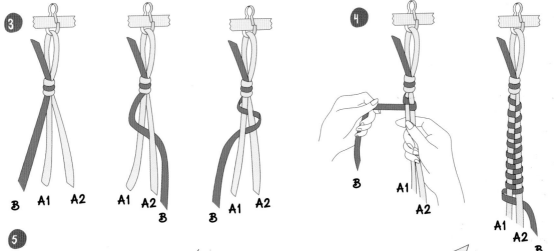

CORKSCREW BRAID BRACELET

If you like a little less structure in your style, try your hand at the corkscrew braid, which has a little bit of a chaotic look to it.

MATERIALS

- 48" (122cm) plastic lace in color A
- 48" (122cm) plastic lace in color B
- Lanyard hook or paper clip
- Tape or safety pin

1. Fold each lace 12" (30.5cm) from the end.

2. Tie an overhand knot ½" (1.5cm) from the fold. Attach a lanyard hook or paper clip to the fold.

3. Tape or pin the hook to a surface, such as the table or the leg of your jeans, to make it easier to braid. Position the short strands (A2 and B2) in the center and the long strands (A1 and B1) on the outside.

4. Bring A1 over both short strands and under B1, forming a loop.

5. Bring B1 under both short strands and up through the loop formed by A1.

6. Keeping the laces flat, pull the long strands tightly to form a knot.

7. Bring B1 over both short strands and under A1, forming a loop.

8. Bring A1 under both short strands and up through the loop formed by B1.

9. Keeping the laces flat, pull the long strands tightly to form a knot. Repeat steps 4—9 until the bracelet fits your wrist.

10. Remove the tape and hook from the loop end of the bracelet. Tie two overhand knots, one on top of the other, with the ends of the lace. Trim the tails.

11. Wrap the bracelet around your wrist and slide the knot into the loop for the closure.

To make a keychain, you will need 24" (61cm) of each color. Make the braid shorter and leave the lanyard hook in place.

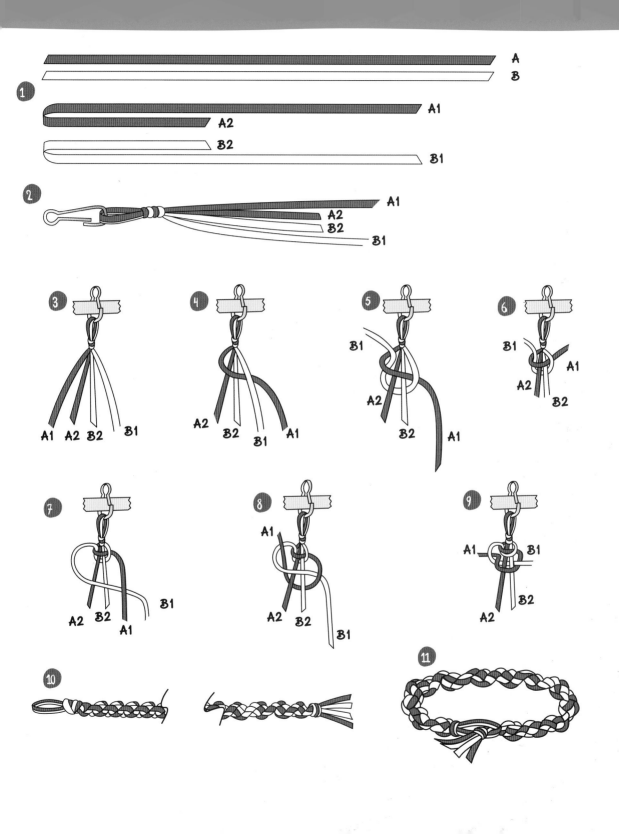

LADDER BRAID BRACELET

The ladder braid creates a very sturdy length of lace that makes it perfect for holding important things like keys.

MATERIALS

- 48" (122cm) plastic lace in color A
- 48" (122cm) plastic lace in color B
- Lanyard hook or paper clip
- Tape or safety pin

1. Fold each lace 12" (30.5cm) from the end.
2. Tie an overhand knot ½" (1.5cm) from the fold. Attach a lanyard hook or paper clip to the fold.
3. Tape or pin the hook to a surface, such as the table or the leg of your jeans, to make it easier to braid. Position the short (A2 and B2) strands in the center and the long strands (A1 and B1) on the outside.
4. Bring A1 over both short strands and under B1, forming a loop.
5. Bring B1 under both short strands and up through the loop formed by A1.
6. Tighten the knot by pulling both long strands.
7. Bring B1 under both short strands and over A1, forming a loop.
8. Bring A1 over both short strands and down through the loop formed by B1.
9. Keeping the laces flat, pull the long strands tightly to form a knot. Repeat steps 4–9 until the bracelet fits your wrist.
10. Remove the tape and hook from the loop end of the bracelet. Tie two overhand knots, one on top of the other, with the ends of the lace. Trim the tails.
11. Wrap the bracelet around your wrist and slide the knot into the loop for the closure.

To make a keychain, you will need 24" (61cm) of each color. Make the braid shorter and leave the lanyard hook in place.

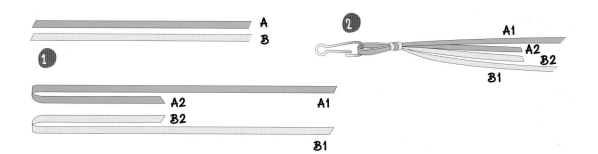

1

A
B

A2   A1
B2
    B1

2

A1
A2
B2
B1

3

A1   A2   B2   B1

4

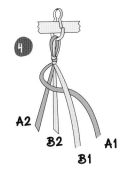

A2
B2   A1
B1

5

B1
A2
B2   A1

6

B1   A1
A2   B2

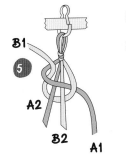

7

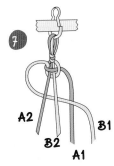

A2
B2   B1
A1

8

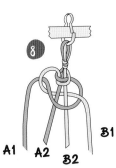

A1   A2   B2   B1

9

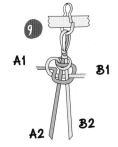

A1   B1
A2   B2

10

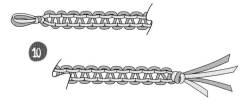

11

SLIPPER BRAID BRACELET

The slipper braid looks like something you spent hours weaving, but it's actually quite simple and fun. Little effort, great result!

MATERIALS

- 2 yards (2m) plastic lace

1. Fold the lace in half.
2. Bring A over B to form a loop.
3. Form part of A into a fold and push it up into the loop. Pull B to form a slipknot.
4. Gently pull A to adjust the size of the knot. Your slipknot should look like this.
5. Form part of B into a fold and push it up into the slipknot to form loop 1.
6. Tighten and close the slip knot by firmly pulling on A. Form part of A into a fold and push it up into loop 1 to form loop 2.
7. Tighten and close loop 1 into a knot by firmly pulling on B.

8. Form part of B into a fold and push it up into loop 2 to form loop 3.
9. Tighten and close loop 2 into a knot by firmly pulling on A.
10. Continue forming loops this way until the bracelet fits your wrist. Finish by forming a loop with strand A as shown and pulling B tight.
11. Pull the end of A all the way out until there are no more loops, just two loose lace ends.
12. Shape the braid into a bracelet.
13. Feed the end of A into the slipknot made at the beginning and thread A back into the loop for B.
14. Push the end of B through the loop you just made with A.
15. Pull A and B to form a tight knot. Trim the tails.

1 A / B

2 B / A

3 B / A

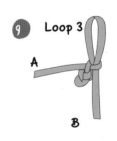

4 A — Slip Knot — B

5 Loop 1 — A — Slip Knot — B

6 Loop 1 — Loop 1 — A — Slip Knot — B / Loop 1 — A — Loop 2 — B

7 A — Loop 2 — B

8 Loop 3 — Loop 2 — A — B

9 Loop 3 — A — B

10 A — B

11 B — A

12 B — A

13 B — A

14 A — B

15

GOD'S EYES

Ojos de Dios, or God's Eyes, are a super popular summer camp craft, but they also have deeper roots in several Mexican and southwestern United States indigenous cultures. The brightly-colored yarns are woven around a cross to form an "eye" shape—often treated as a symbol of the all-seeing supreme creator.

MATERIALS FOR SMALL VERSION

- 9 feet (275cm) green plastic lace
- 8 feet (245cm) yellow plastic lace
- 7 feet (215cm) red plastic lace
- 2 dowels, ⅜" (1cm) wide and 5" (12.5cm) long
- 26-gauge floral wire
- Tape
- Craft knife

MATERIALS FOR LARGE VERSION

- 40 feet (12.2m) black plastic lace
- 17 feet (5.2m) turquoise plastic lace
- 15 feet (4.6m) white plastic lace
- 13 feet (4m) red plastic lace
- 2 dowels, ⅜" (1cm) wide and 10" (25.5cm) long
- 26-gauge floral wire
- Tape
- Craft knife

1. Use a craft knife to carefully notch the center of two dowels. Match the notches and cross one dowel over the other to form an X. Wrap floral wire in an X shape over the center of the dowels to hold them together.

2. Wrap lace over the center of the dowels in an X shape and tape it down.

3. Start with the first color of lace, taping one end to the dowel in the center. Wrap the lace counter-clockwise over and around the dowels as shown in the diagram, forming a square. Do not twist the lace as you go. Pull each row tight and push it against the previous rows.

4. To change the color, tape the end of the original piece of lace to the underside of the dowel. Then tape the beginning of the next piece of lace in the new color to the underside of the dowel at the same spot, and continue wrapping.

5. To make the small version, wrap the lace in the following order: green center, three rows green, three rows yellow, three rows red, two rows green, two rows red, four rows yellow, three rows green.

6. To make the large version, wrap the lace in the following order: red center, eight rows red, five rows black, six rows turquoise, three rows black, four rows white, three rows black, three rows red, three rows black, five rows turquoise, three rows black, two rows white, two rows black.

7. When you are finished wrapping, tape down the end of the last piece of lace.

8. To make a hanger, thread a piece of lace under the wrapped lace at the tip of a dowel. Bring the ends together and tie an overhand knot.

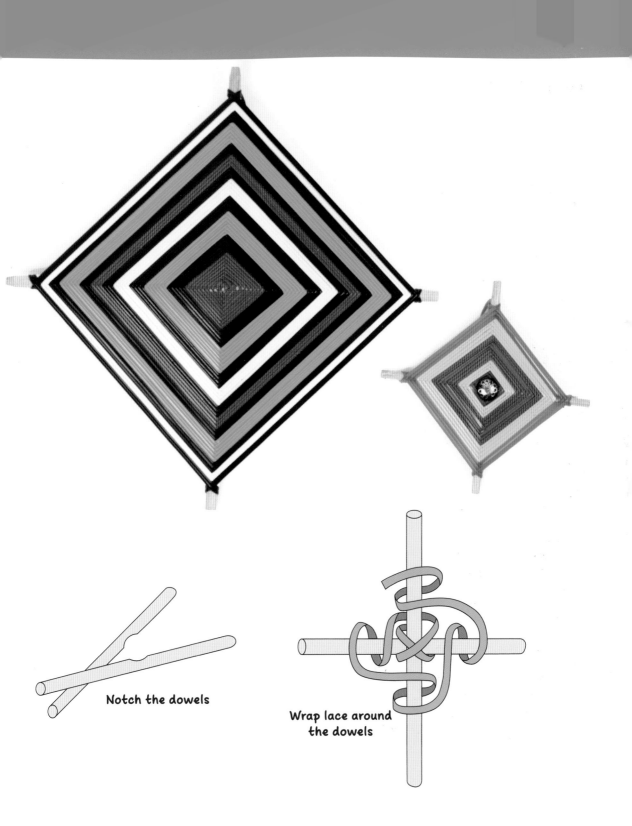

Notch the dowels

**Wrap lace around
the dowels**

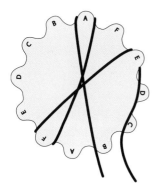

Peg F ⟶ Peg E
Peg D ⟶ Peg C
Peg B ⟶ Peg A
Peg F ⟶ Peg E
Peg D ⟶ Peg C
Peg B ⟶ Peg A
    (starting point)

LOOPY FLOWERS

Create simple and colorful flower shapes by wrapping lace around a special wheel. How much plastic lace you'll need depends on how big you want your flower to be.

MATERIALS

- 5 or 10 yards (4.5 or 9m) plastic lace for petals
- 1 or 2 yards (1 or 2m) plastic lace for center
- Plastic tapestry needle
- Flower wheel (or scrap piece of sturdy cardboard)
- Glue

1. If you don't have a plastic flower wheel like the one used here, you can make your own. Photocopy the wheel pattern from the first diagram to be 3" (7.5cm) for a small flower or 4" (10cm) for a large flower. Trace and cut out the wheel from a piece of sturdy cardboard (such as from a real box, not a flimsy cereal box). Label the edges with letters as shown.

2. Hold the wheel with the letters facing you and an A at the top. Keep this A at the top the entire time you are wrapping. Wrap the long lace around A to start with a little extra hanging down the center in front of the wheel, then follow the chart (see bottom left), always wrapping around the letter that is farther away from where you currently are (not next to where you currently are).

3. When you are back at the first peg A, you have completed one round. Repeat the same sequence for four or five rounds.

4. When you are done with the petals, weave the end of the lace into the back of the flower (between the flower and the wheel) to secure it. Use the needle if you need to.

5. Weave one end of the short lace into the back of the flower to secure it (using the needle if you need to). Bring the lace to the front of the flower.

6. Pass the lace over two and back under one set of strands as shown, going all the way around until you have filled in the flower center to your desired size. Use the needle if you need to.

7. Weave the end of the short lace into the back of the flower to secure it.

8. Remove the flower from the wheel and make sure all the lace ends are well secured. Trim excess lace as needed. Apply a drop of glue to the lace ends.

RUBBER Bands

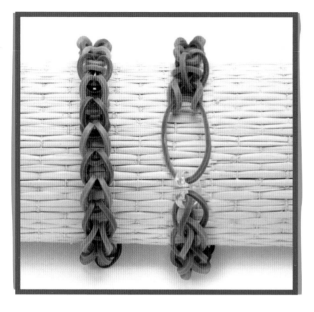

BASIC LOOM BRACELET

This basic bracelet introduces you to the loom and the general idea of placing bands and looping them. If you've never made rubber band projects on a loom before, you should start here to get the hang of it, then try your hand at some more cool projects! Check out the helpful diagram on page 105 as you follow these step-by-step instructions.

MATERIALS

- 25 rubber bands (for this example, 13 purple and 12 pink)
- 1 plastic clip
- Rubber band loom
- Rubber band hook

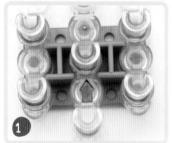

1 Turn your loom so that the arrow faces **up** (away from you); the bottom middle peg sticks out at the bottom.

2 Place your first rubber band on the bottom middle peg (the one closest to you) and stretch it onto the bottom right peg.

3 Place your second rubber band on the peg you just ended on and stretch it onto the peg to the upper left (the middle peg second from the bottom).

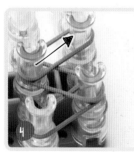

4 Place your third rubber band on the peg you just ended on and stretch it onto the peg to the upper right of it.

5 Keep on repeating this back-and-forth pattern until you've run out of bands or reached the top of the loom. **Always remember to start on the last peg you ended on.** Now look at the diagram and photo on page 105 and make sure that your loom looks like the pictures.

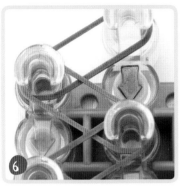

6. Now you are ready to loop! First, turn your loom so that the arrow at the top is facing **down** (towards you).

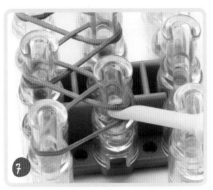

7. Starting at the bottom of the loom (closest to you), **push your hook down into the big loop** created by the last band you placed. Hook the second-to-last band you placed, being sure to hook it **inside the groove** on the peg.

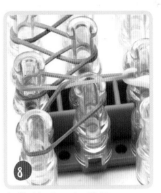

8. Lift the band off the bottom middle peg...

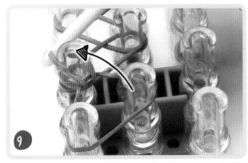

9. ...and loop it around the peg to the upper left, which is the other peg that the band is also looped on. This is looping a band back to the peg it came from.

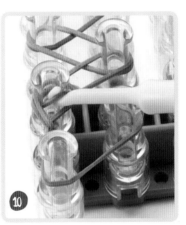

10. Now, push your hook down into the groove in the peg you just looped onto, and hook the next rubber band. Don't hook the one you just looped!

NEVER DO THIS!

Never hook a band by going around the outside as shown in this photo. **ALWAYS** push your hook down into the groove of the peg you are on, down inside the bands that are already looped there, as shown in step 10.

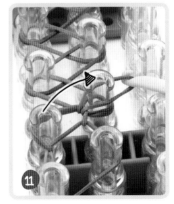

11. Lift the band off the peg and loop it back to the peg it came from.

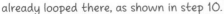

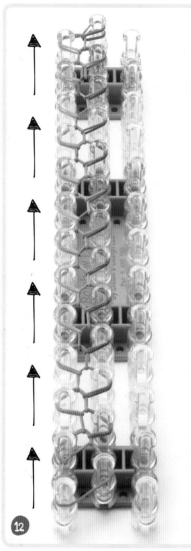

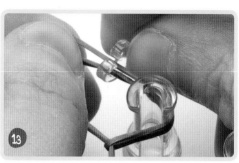

13 Take your clip and hook it around **both strands** of the one rubber band that is looped on the top middle peg, the very last band that you looped. It helps to pull the strands taut with one finger.

14 Holding the clip firmly between your fingers, pull the bracelet off the loom, one peg at a time. Don't be afraid to pull hard; it won't break!

15 Clip the rubber band on the other end onto the clip. You've made your first bracelet!

12 Keep on repeating this pattern all the way up to the top of the loom. **Always remember to push your hook down into the groove before hooking the next band.** Here's what your loom should look like after you finish all the looping! Stick with it; soon it'll become like second nature!

UNDERSTANDING DIAGRAMS

Now that you've made a basic bracelet, look at the diagram for the basic bracelet so that you will be able to use the other rubber band diagrams in this book. The diagram shows you the order in which you must place your rubber bands and how your loom will look once you have finished placing all the bands. This is called loading the loom. After loading the loom, follow the step-by-step instructions to make the project.

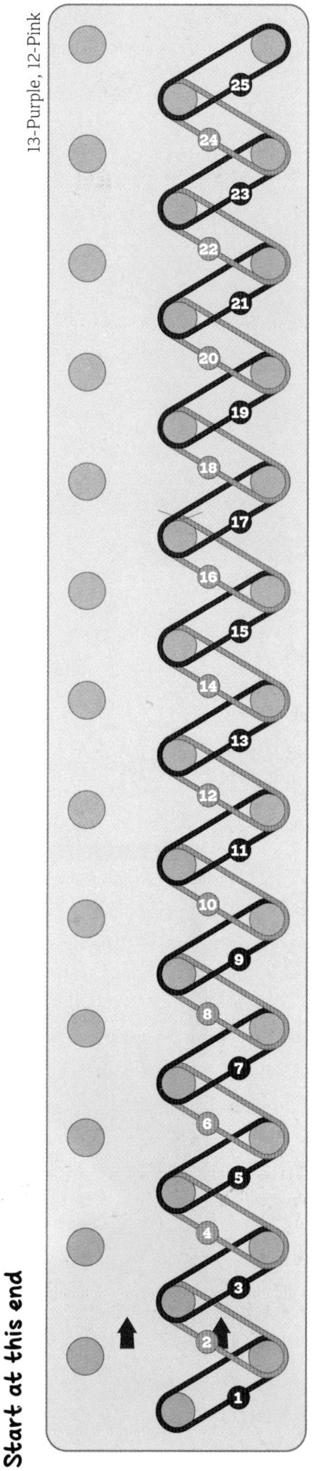
13-Purple, 12-Pink
Start at this end
1
2
3
4
5
6
7
8
9
10
11
12
13
14
15
16
17
18
19
20
21
22
23
24
25

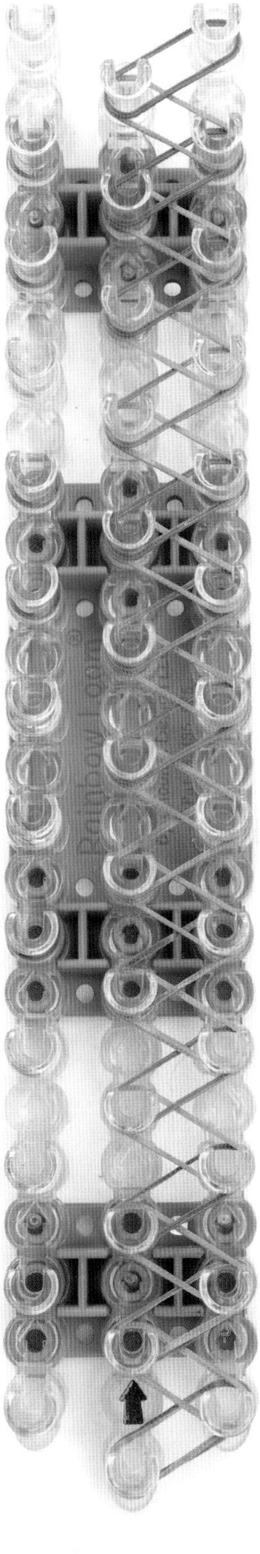

FRINGE BRACELET/ SCRUNCHIE

This super simple accessory can be used as a bracelet or as a hair scrunchie! It's made with two columns of bands connected by horizontal bands that aren't looped.

MATERIALS

- 39 black rubber bands (for base)
- 1 black rubber band (to finish)
- 104 purple rubber bands (for fringe)
- 1 plastic clip
- Rubber band loom
- Rubber band hook

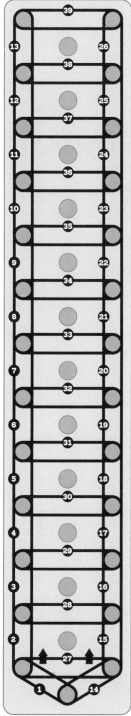

LOADING DIAGRAM

Place the side columns (bands 1–26) first, then place the horizontal stripe bands starting near the bottom of the loom (bands 27–39). You'll be adding the fringe bands as you loop.

1

Turn the loom so the arrow faces down. Place four loose bands onto your hook near the tip.

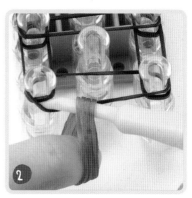

2

Holding the loose bands out of the way, push your hook down into the bottom left peg to hook the bottom band from inside the stripe band.

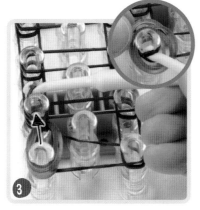

3

Slide the four loose bands down off the hook and onto the peg. Now loop the band you have hooked up to the peg above it. This pulls the link all the way through the four loose bands.

4

Repeat this process for all the links on both columns, adding four loose bands to every link, including when you loop the bands from the top left and right pegs onto the top middle peg. Knot the top bands together using a lark's head knot (see page 112), pull the piece off the loom, clip the ends together, and you're done!

VINE BRACELET

This bracelet is super customizable! You can add beads, double or triple the bands, and even twist the bands in various ways to create many different bracelets with just one design. Have fun with it!

MATERIALS

- 34 pink rubber bands (for vine)
- 10, 20, or 30 lime green rubber bands (for rings)
- 1 plastic clip
- Rubber band loom
- Rubber band hook

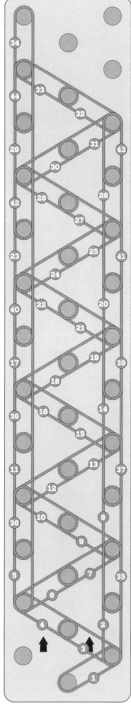

LOADING DIAGRAM

First, place the 34 "vine" bands as shown in the diagram. It's like a zigzag, but with an extra up-and-down band at each corner. Make sure you place the extra up-and-down band first before continuing to zig and zag to the left and right. Once you've placed all 34 vine bands, add the "ring" bands where shown to fill in the holes, starting with band 35 near the bottom of the loom. You can use one, two, three, or more bands at once for the ring bands—it's up to you! (The diagram shows a single ring band design.)

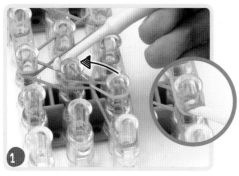

Turn the loom so the arrow faces down. Hook the bottom band on the second from bottom right peg and loop it up to the second from bottom middle peg. Be sure to push your hook down into the peg, inside the last ring band you placed, to hook the band.

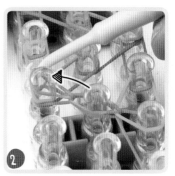

Push your hook down into the peg and hook the bottom band on the second from bottom middle peg, where you just ended. Loop it to the peg to the upper left of it.

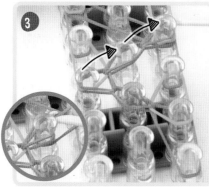

Then, starting from the peg you just ended on, loop the next two bottom bands diagonally up and to the right, like you did in steps 1—2.

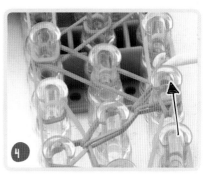

Now loop the band from the third from bottom right peg up to the fourth from bottom right peg. This is the band that shares a peg with the top of the ring band closest to you. The ring bands do not get looped.

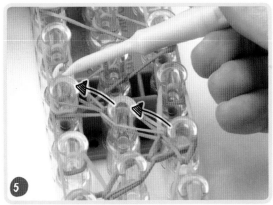

5

Now, starting from the peg you just ended on, loop the next two bottom bands, diagonally up and to the left, like you did in step 3. The first band goes from the right column to the center column; the second band goes from the center column to the left column.

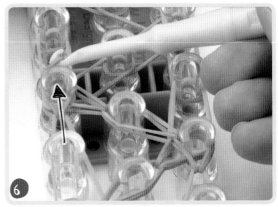

6

As in step 4, loop the band that shares a peg with the top of the second ring band up to the peg above it. This is looping the band from the fourth from bottom left peg to the fifth from bottom left peg.

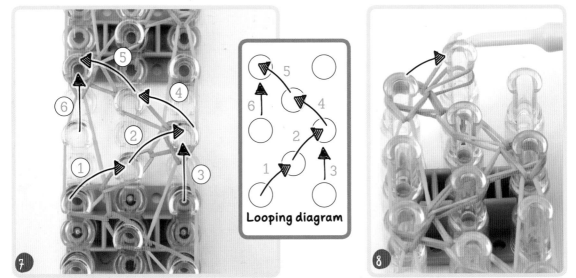

Looping diagram

7

Repeat the pattern in steps 3–6 for the rest of the bracelet, following the zigzag path you made when you placed the bands. Always loop two bands diagonally up and across ① ②, then loop up the band that connects the next ring band ③. Use the looping diagram as a guide.

8

Loop the bottom band from the top left peg to the top middle peg, add a clip, and pull your bracelet off the loom.

Start at this end

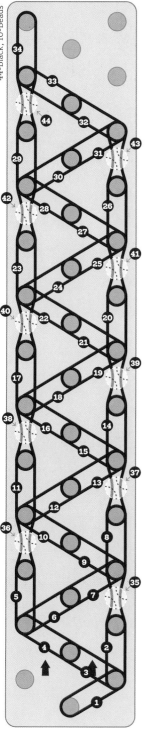

Baseball Beads: To make a beaded vine bracelet, simply add a pony bead or other bead to each ring band before placing the ring bands on the loom.

Start at this end

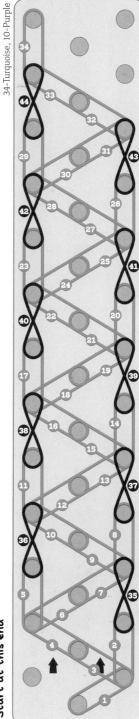

Figure Eights: Figure eights are a lot of fun! When placing the ring bands on the loom, twist them once to make a figure eight between the two pegs the ring bands are stretched on. That's all there is to it!

CELL PHONE COVER

This spiffy cell phone cover will jazz up the basic black or white of many phones, make the phone more grippy to prevent dropping, and doesn't block most buttons, headphone jacks, or selfie cameras! You'll be creating two separate panel pieces and then "stitching" them together. It's a challenge, but it's fun! To make this project, you will need to combine two looms with the pegs in an alternating pattern, exactly as shown in the loading diagram. (You can't just place two looms next to one another and not change the peg columns around—that won't work.)

MATERIALS

- 144 blue rubber bands (72 per loom load)
- 96 white rubber bands (48 per loom load)
- 46 green rubber bands (to stitch)
- 1 green rubber band (to finish)
- 13 plastic clips
- 2 rubber band looms
- Rubber band hook

MAKING A LARK'S HEAD KNOT WITH RUBBER BANDS

Push your hook through all the bands you want to connect. Grab a new band (a finishing band) and hook it onto the hook. Slide the other end of the band securely around your finger. Pull the hook end of the band through all the bands. Loop the band on your finger onto the hook, placing it behind the band that's already there and holding it down against the hook with one finger. Grab the front loop—the one that is closest to the hook end of the hook—and slide it onto one finger, then pull it off the hook, keeping it on your finger. Now slide the remaining loop off the hook (shown in photo), and pull the loop on your finger to tighten the knot.

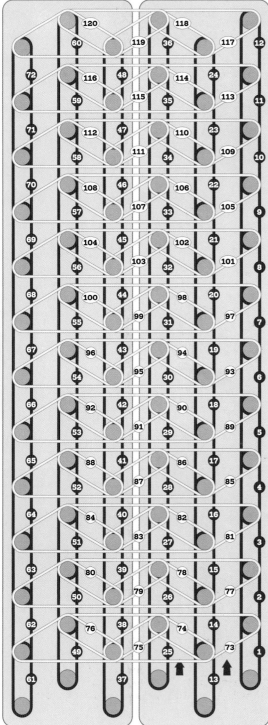

Start at this end

LOADING DIAGRAM

Make sure your connected looms look exactly like the diagram, with the pegs all staggered. First load all of the bands up each of the six columns (bands 1–72). Then add the connecting triangle bands around three pegs, one at a time. Notice that you start on the bottom right side with a triangle whose point faces down (band 73); then place the next triangle with its point facing up (band 74); then the next triangle with its point facing down (band 75); then the last triangle in the row with its point facing up (band 76). See the illustration below to help you understand.

Bands 1–72

Bands 73–120
See below:
Overlapping Triangles

Overlapping Triangles

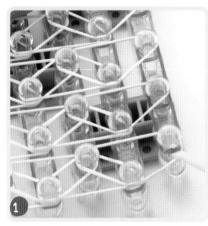

1

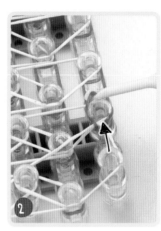

2

3

Turn the loom so the arrow faces down. Hook the bottom band on the bottom right peg, making sure to push your hook down into the groove (inside the triangle band).

Loop the band to the peg directly above it.

Loop the entire right column this way, always making sure to push your hook down into the groove, inside the triangle bands. When you finish the column, clip the final band on the top peg.

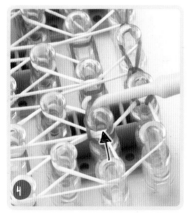

4

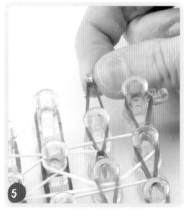

5

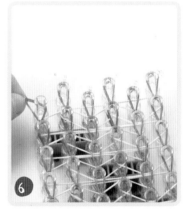

6

Go to the bottom peg on the second from right column. Hook the bottom band on that peg, making sure to push your hook down into the groove, inside the triangle bands. Loop it to the peg directly above it.

Loop the entire column this way, always making sure to push your hook down into the groove, inside the triangle bands. When you finish the column, clip the final band on the top peg.

Hook and loop all four remaining columns this way, clipping the final band at the top of each column. Always make sure to push your hook down into the groove, inside the triangle bands.

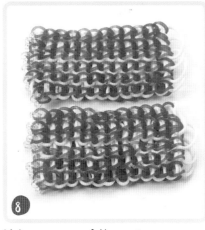

Carefully pull the piece off the loom, going one peg at a time until you can get a good grip on all the bands at once. Set the piece aside.

Make one more of these pieces as you did in steps 1–7. Then align the two pieces together as shown, with all the clipped ends to the left. If you are left handed, you may want to reverse the directions in these instructions to make it easier to do.

Push your hook up through the two middle links on the far right (non-clipped side). This is one link from each piece. Make sure you push your hook through all four loops of the two links. (With the piece lying flat, you should be pushing your hook through the four strands of the two links that are visible on top.)

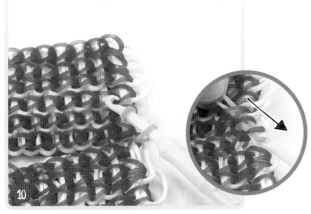

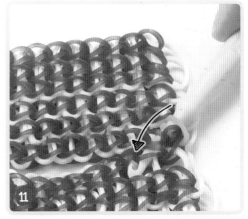

Pull a new "stitch" band through all four loops on your hook, and put the other end of the band on your hook. You've created a new link that connects the two pieces.

Your hook should be facing up. Without dropping the stitch link that is on the hook, turn your hook so that it faces down (hold the pieces down on the table), and push it through all four loops of the next two links in the row, one link from each piece.

Create another new connecting stitch link as in step 10, but be sure you pull the link through all **six** loops on the hook, including the two loops of the first stitch link you made.

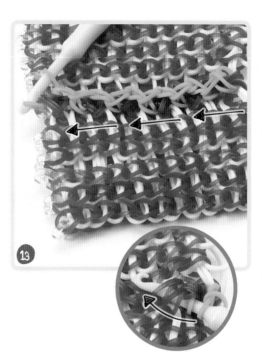

Repeat this process for all the links along the two middle rows to stitch the two pieces together. Alternate going up through the links and down through the links. Whenever you complete a stitch and your hook is facing down (as after step 12), turn your hook and push it **up** through the next two links (inset); whenever you complete a stitch and your hook is facing up (as after step 10), turn your hook and push it **down** through the next two links.

When you get all the way to the end of the middle rows, on the left side, add a clip to your last stitch link. You will have made 12 stitches total. Remove your hook.

Now look at all 12 clipped links that are along the left side. There are six on each piece, and you already linked together the two clipped links in the middle, one from each piece. You'll now be stitching these 12 links together and getting rid of the clips.

Push your hook up through the last (clipped) stitch you made in step 14, and up through the first (bottom) link of the top piece. Make sure you push your hook through **all four loops**, since you will be taking the clips off.

Make a connecting link through all the bands on the hook.

Remove the clip on the link you just connected to the stitch link to make sure that you connected them correctly. If it doesn't start to fall apart, you did it right. Leave the stitch link clipped for now.

One by one, stitch together the remaining five links on the top piece. Always push your hook through the next link up from the bottom, as shown. Always pull the new connecting link through all four loops on the hook. You'll make five more stitches this way. Remove the clips as you go. Then clip the final stitch at the top and take your hook out.

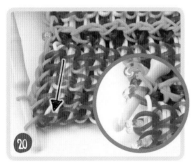

Repeat this stitching pattern for the bottom piece, starting in the middle with the stitch band you left clipped in step 14 and working your way down. When you reach the bottom, keep your hook through the last connecting link at the bottom.

Now it's time to cinch the top and bottom with connecting stitches. **Turn your piece 180 degrees** so that you are starting with your hook at the top right instead of the bottom left.

Without dropping the link on your hook (your hook should be facing up), turn your hook down and push it down through, not the link right next to it along the top, but the link **after that**—you are **skipping** a link. With the piece lying flat, you should be pushing your hook through the two strands of the link that are visible on top.

Create a connecting link through all four loops on your hook. Skipping links like this is what will tighten the phone cover.

Continue stitching along the top by skipping every other link. Alternate pushing your hook up through the links and down through the links, as described in step 13. So, to make your second stitch along the top, you should push your hook up through the link, as shown.

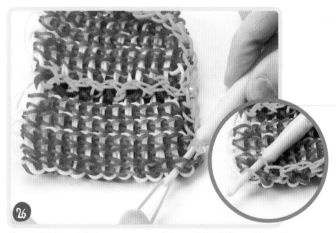

You'll make a total of six stitches along the top. **The last stitch will have to be right next to the link you just stitched,** because there is an even number of links to be stitched. Clip the last stitch and remove your hook.

Repeat this stitching process (steps 22–25) on the other end of the piece, starting from the bottom right where you clipped a stitch, and starting with your hook facing down through the clipped stitch and the second link (you skip the first). **Be sure to remember to alternate links.**

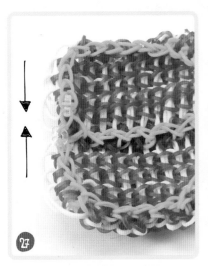

Now, from the top down and the bottom up, create connecting stitches between all 12 links on the remaining open side, as you did in steps 16–20 on the other side that was clipped. Make sure that you make these stitches through both of the loops of the links, as you did on the other side. You'll make 10 stitches this way (five from the top down and five from the bottom up).

Where the two final connecting stitches meet in the middle, push your hook through all **12** bands that the two clipped stitches connect together.

NOTE:

For the fifth stitch on each half, push your hook through the very first stitch you made in step 10 before pushing your hook through the middle link. Then make a stitch through all six loops on the hook. This will make the case tighter.

Knot all these bands together with a lark's head knot (see page 112) and remove the clipped stitches.

Cut off the eight extra ring bands and remove any clips that are still on the cell phone cover.

Fit your new cell phone case onto your phone!

GENERAL PONY BEAD ANIMAL CRAFTING TIPS

Review these basic instructions for making pony bead animals, then dive right in with any of your favorite species on the following pages!

Getting Started

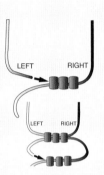

1. Cut the cord you are going to use, find the center, and mount it on a key ring or lanyard hook with a lark's head knot. Or you can fold the cord in half and tie an overhand knot to create a loop. If desired, you can wrap the ends of your cord with tape to make a point or dip the ends in white glue and let dry to prevent fraying.
2. String beads for the first row of a project onto the right cord. Weave the left cord through the beads from left to right. Slide the beads all the way up so they are snug against the first knot.
3. String the second row of beads onto the new right cord. Weave the left cord through the beads from left to right. Slide the beads all the way up so they are snug against the previous row.
4. Continue this way to create the entire body of the animal.

Basic Arms, Legs, and Wings

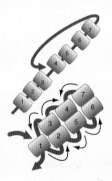

To incorporate arms, legs, and wings into the main body of the animal using the main body cords, follow these directions. String all the beads for each appendage onto one of the body cords. Push the beads for the outermost row a little bit farther out on the cord, then push the beads for the next-to-last row a little bit farther out too. Weave the cord back through the beads for the next-to-last row and pull to tighten. Push the beads for the next row out and weave the cord through them. Continue until the arm, leg, or wing construction is complete. Beginning at the body, pull the cord through, one row at a time, to tighten the cord and bring the arm, leg, or wing up against the body.

Special Arms, Legs, and Wings

Construct ears, arms, legs, tails, and wings as needed following the individual project instructions. You can also use wire in place of cord to make poseable animals and dolls.

Finishing

After beading is complete, tie the cord ends in one or two overhand knots to secure the beads. If beads are added to the ending cord, tie another knot to secure all added beads.

Support Thread

Occasionally a beaded piece will be loose, especially when the beads are strung on a soft ribbon or yarn or when the cords are not pulled taut. Simply weave an extra cord up through the center beads to bulk out the main cord and make the piece stiffer.

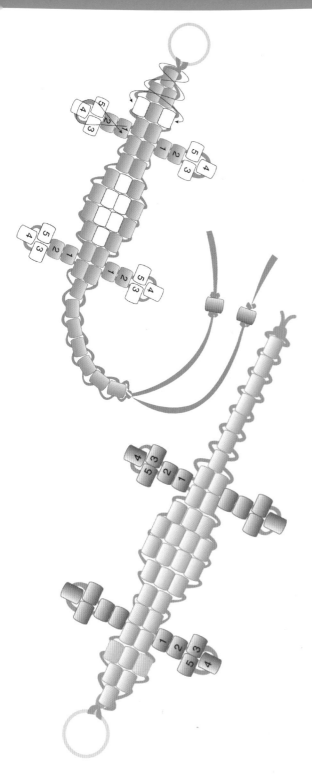

GREEN AND WHITE GECKO

- Pony beads: 37 green, 20 white, 2 red
- Cord: 2 yards (2m) of white ribbon
- Start: lark's head knot and split ring
- Finish: overhand knot and long tails with
  added beads

BLUE GECKO

- Pony beads: 27 light blue, 6 aqua, 20 brown,
  2 orange
- Cord: 2 yards (2m) of aqua rattail (satin) cord
- Start: lark's head knot and split ring (or overhand
  knot with loop as shown in photo)
- Finish: overhand knot

WATERMELON

Project by Delores Frantz

- Pony beads: 48 red, 26 green, 19 white, 5 black
- Cord: 2 yards (2m) of green plastic lace
- Start: lark's head knot and split ring (or lanyard hook as shown in photo)
- Finish: overhand knots

KITE

Project by Virginia Reynolds

- Pony beads: 48 red, 14 green, 13 yellow
- Cord: 2 yards (2m) of red plastic lace
- Start: lark's head knot and split ring (or lanyard hook as shown in photo)
- Finish: Make the kite tail with the loose cord ends as shown.

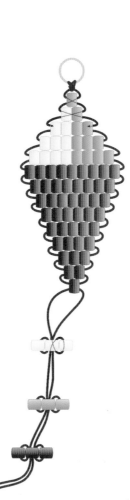

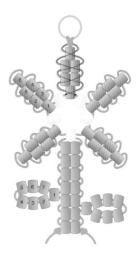

FLOWER

Project by Dawn Maier

- Pony beads: 30 neon pink, 28 neon green, 5 neon yellow
- Cord: 2 yards (2m) of pink round plastic lace
- Start: lark's head knot and split ring (or overhand knot with loop as shown in photo). Make the circle first, then add the petals.
- Finish: overhand knots

DOG

- Pony beads: 79 rust, 53 tan, 27 dark brown, 9 white, 2 black
- Cord: 3 yards (3m) of brown plastic lace

LEOPARD

- Pony beads: 98 yellow, 46 black, 3 brown
- Cord: 3 yards (3m) of yellow plastic lace
- Ears: After completing row 5, add two black beads to each cord. Bring the left cord through beads 3, 2, and 1 and the right cord through beads 4, 5, and 6.

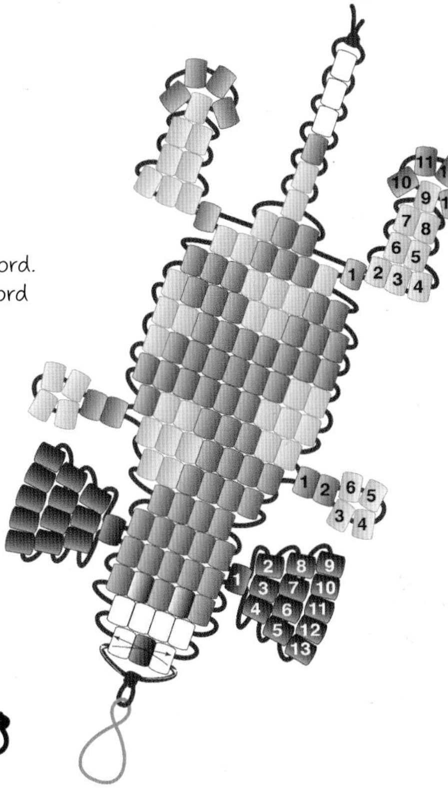

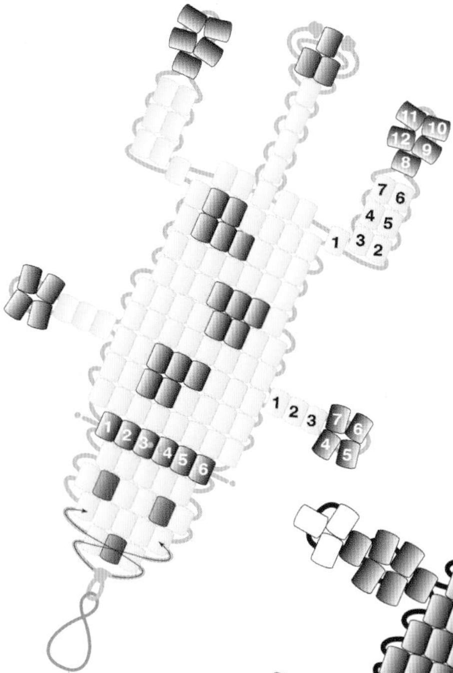

Leopard Ears

All projects, unless otherwise noted, are started with a ring and finished with overhand knots.

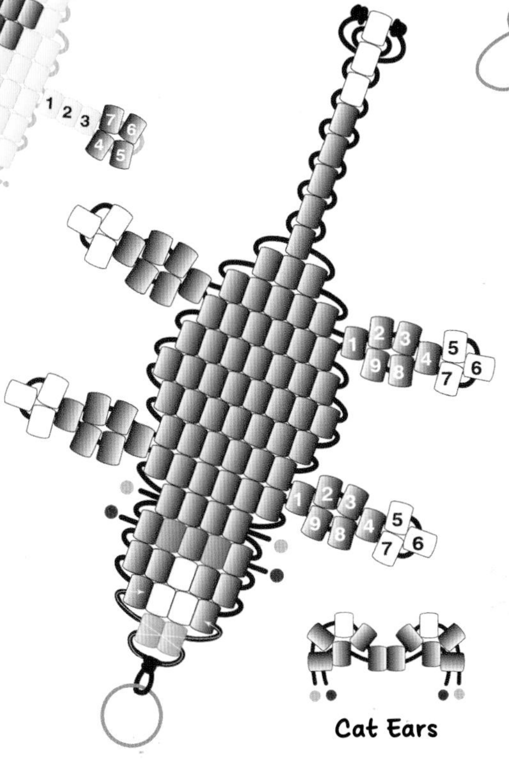

CAT

- Pony beads: 99 black, 20 white, 2 blue, 2 pink
- Cord: 3 yards (3m) of black plastic lace

Cat Ears

All projects, unless otherwise noted, are started with a lanyard hook and finished with overhand knots.

CORAL SNAKE

- Pony beads: 22 black, 17 red, 15 yellow
- Cord: 2 yards (2m) of black yarn

RATTLESNAKE

- Pony beads: 2 red, 31 tan, 15 rust, 8 gray
- Cord: 2 yards (2m) of tan yarn

HAPPY FACE

- Pony beads: 34 yellow, 10 black
- Cord: 2 yards (2m) of yellow yarn

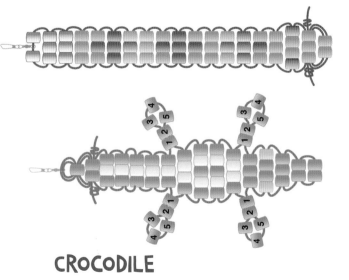

CROCODILE

- Pony beads: 55 green, 13 green pearl, 2 orange crystal
- Cord: 2 yards (2m) of green yarn

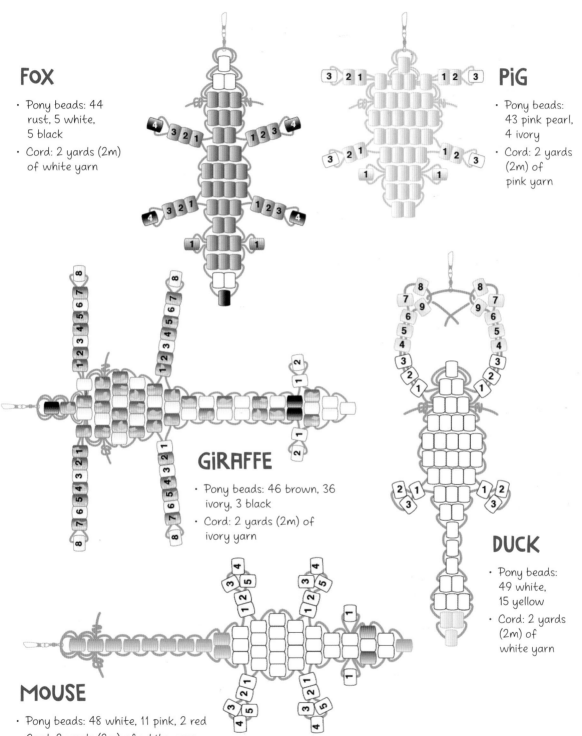

FOX

- Pony beads: 44 rust, 5 white, 5 black
- Cord: 2 yards (2m) of white yarn

PIG

- Pony beads: 43 pink pearl, 4 ivory
- Cord: 2 yards (2m) of pink yarn

GiRAFFE

- Pony beads: 46 brown, 36 ivory, 3 black
- Cord: 2 yards (2m) of ivory yarn

DUCK

- Pony beads: 49 white, 15 yellow
- Cord: 2 yards (2m) of white yarn

MOUSE

- Pony beads: 48 white, 11 pink, 2 red
- Cord: 2 yards (2m) of white yarn

TOUCAN

Project by Dawn Maier

- Pony beads: 50 black, 7 yellow, 13 neon orange, 4 neon yellow, 5 neon green, 24 white
- Cord: 2 yards (2m) of black round plastic lace
- Start: overhand knot and lanyard hook
- Beak: Add neon orange, neon green, and neon yellow beads and form the beak shape. Go back through the neon green, the neon orange, and the neon green again before adding the next row.
- Finish: overhand knots

FROG

- Pony beads: 29 green (body), 30 neon green (legs), 12 orange, 9 red, 2 black
- Cord: 2 yards (2m) of green plastic lace
- Start: overhand knot with loop
- Finish: overhand knots

DRAGONFLY

Project by Virginia Reynolds

- Pony beads: 42 silver glitter, 9 neon pink, 4 neon blue
- Cord: 2 yards (2m) clear plastic lace
- Start: overhand knot with loop
- Finish: overhand knot and long tails with added beads

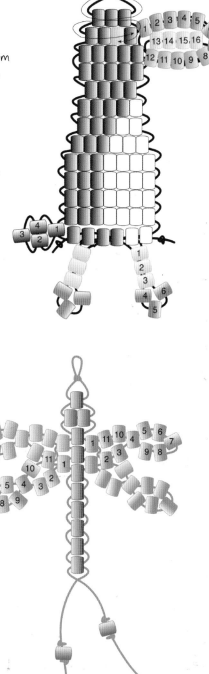

Coiled Wire Bracelets

TWO-BAND BRACELETS

Project by Melissa Devenport

If you want a functional pony bead accessory, why not incorporate a watch? Or, if you like the look of colorful tiles, include those for a super decorative bracelet.

MATERIALS FOR WATCH VERSION

- 36–52 pony beads
- Watch face
- 2 pieces of stretchy 15" (38cm) cord
- Glue

MATERIALS FOR PHOTO/ TILE VERSION

- 44 pony beads
- 2 side-drilled bracelet photo frames or
- 2 side-drilled tiles/ dominoes
- 2 pieces of stretchy 15" (38cm) cord
- Glue

To make the watch version, first pass a cord through one side of the watch and center it. String nine to thirteen beads on each side of the cord. Tie the two ends together with a double overhand knot and secure it with glue. Tuck the cord tails inside the beads. Repeat with the other cord on the other side of the watch.

To make the photo/tile version, first string seven beads onto one cord. Pass the cord through the top hole of a photo frame/tile. String on six beads. Pass the cord through the top hole of the second photo frame/tile. String on seven beads. Tie the two ends together with a double overhand knot and secure it with glue. Tuck the cord tails inside the beads. Repeat with the other cord, passing it through the bottom holes of the photo frames/tiles. Glue photos into the photo frames.

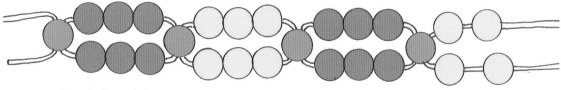

Loops Bracelet

LOOPS BRACELET

You'll love playing with the loops on this bracelet. Who needs a fidget spinner when you have a cool accessory like this?

MATERIALS

- 8 pony beads of Color A
- 24 pony beads of Color B
- 18 pony beads of Color C
- 2 pieces of stretchy 15" (38cm) cord
- Glue

1. Tie the two cords together with an overhand knot, leaving 3" (7.5cm) tails.
2. Pass both cords through a Color A bead. Separate the cords.
3. String three Color B beads onto each cord. Pass both cords through a Color A bead. Cross the cords and pull gently to tighten the beads. Separate the cords.
4. String three Color C beads onto each cord. Pass both cords through a Color A bead. Cross the cords and pull gently to tighten the beads. Separate the cords.
5. Continue repeating steps 3—4, alternating colors. Adjust the number of beads so the bracelet will fit comfortably.
6. Tie the cord ends together with a double overhand knot. Tuck the cord tails into the beads, adding a drop of glue if desired.

COILED WIRE BRACELET

Project by Melissa Devenport

You really can't get any easier, cheaper, or faster than this bracelet. Simply cut lengths of memory wire, loop on beads, close off the ends, and pop it on your wrist! It's the work of minutes.

MATERIALS

- Bracelet memory wire
- Pony beads for aqua version: 85 aqua, 9 copper, 9 brown, 9 tan, 9 peach, 9 pink
- Pony beads for primary colors version:
- 40 black, 32 red, 32 yellow, 32 green
- Wire cutters or old scissors
- Needle-nose pliers

1. Cut a piece of memory wire so you have four loops for each bracelet. Use the pliers to turn a loop in one end of the wire so the beads don't fall off.
2. To make the aqua version, string the beads in the following order: five aqua, three copper, five aqua, three tan, five aqua, three pink, five aqua, three brown, five aqua, three peach. Repeat until you run out of beads.
3. To make the primary colors version, string the beads in the following order: eight black, eight green, eight yellow, eight red. Repeat until you run out of beads.
4. To finish the bracelet, turn another loop in the other end of the wire.

fusible Beads

GENERAL FUSIBLE BEAD CRAFTING TIPS

Basic Fusing Instructions

1. First, gather your supplies. Reference your chosen pattern and assemble the bead colors necessary, the pegboard(s) called for, tweezers if you have them, an iron, and ironing paper (or parchment paper). Heat up your iron to medium-high heat without steam.

2. Assemble the beads on your board, setting each bead onto the corresponding peg following the chart. Going row by row is good for beginners; going color by color is a little harder, but much faster.

3. Take your completed pegboard to a flat ironing surface. Place ironing paper over the beads. Run the hot iron in slow circles over the paper for about 5—10 seconds at a time. The beads should melt enough that you can see them sticking to the paper.

4. Let the beads cool completely (about 5—10 minutes) before continuing. For large pieces that tend to curl (or just for extra insurance), rest a few heavy books on top of the beads while they cool so the finished piece is nice and flat.

5. Remove the piece from the paper and pegboard. Flip it over and place it back onto the ironing surface (you no longer need the pegboard). Rest the paper back on top of the beads and iron the piece again the same way you did in step 3. Once again, allow the piece to cool.

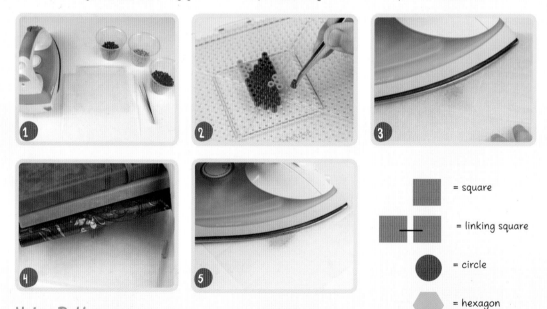

= square

= linking square

= circle

= hexagon

= 5-point star

Using Patterns

Each pattern lists the type of pegboard you'll need and the number of beads in each color used in the design. A symbol represents the type of pegboard; check out this symbol guide. So, for example, if you see " ▇ 1 ", that means you need one square pegboard to make the design.

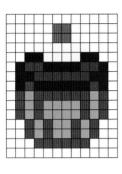

CUPCAKE RING

- ■ 1
- 12 crème
- 4 magenta
- 22 brown
- 10 light brown
- 32 purple
- 22 pastel lavender

Treat yourself to something sweet! Glue designs to ring blanks to keep your favorite bead creations at your fingertips. Mini beads are great for these designs.

HEXAGON CHAIN EARRINGS

- ⬡ 1
- 24 silver
- 24 pearl blue
- ◎ 24 white

Use jump rings to attach a bead creation to a pair of earring hooks for an easy accessory to match any outfit. To make the special hexagon chain earrings shown here, fuse the hexagons, but link them together by cutting the join between two beads in two of the hexagons and gluing them back together once they're interlocked.

HEXAGON BROOCH

- ⬡ 1
- 70 silver
- 14 toothpaste
- 14 pastel lavender

Glue a pin back to your finished piece to create a pinnable work of art for your bag, hat, or shirt collar.

COFFEE CUP

- ■ 1
- ◎ 7 white
- ● 6 brown
- 5 light brown
- 28 tan
- 28 sand

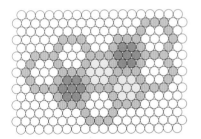

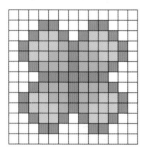

CLOVER

 1

- 41 dark green
- 28 pastel green
- 24 green

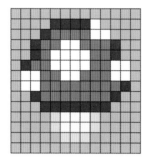

MUSHROOM

1

- 23 white
- 36 hot coral
- 20 red
- 7 sand
- 6 crème

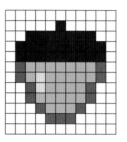

ACORN

1

- 26 dark brown
- 13 light brown
- 25 tan
- 2 sand

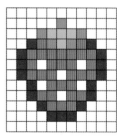

STRAWBERRY

1

- 4 green
- 5 dark green
- 17 red
- 30 hot coral
- 6 white

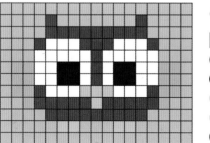

OWL

1

- 40 rust
- 34 white
- 14 tan
- 8 cheddar
- 8 black

Charm Bracelet: Bring the woods with you everywhere you go with this set of five charms. Attach them to a 7" (18cm) chain using five jump rings and then add a clasp. The ones here are made with mini fusible beads, not the standard size.

Cell Phone Charm: Latch a favorite design to a cell phone lanyard for some spot-on cell phone charm. Or use it as a zipper pull for a bag or jacket so everyone can see your style from a distance.

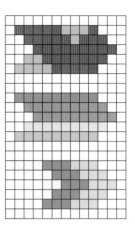

ARROWHEADS

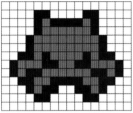

PURPLE BADDIE

 1
● 52 black
◉ 52 plum

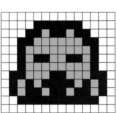

GREEN BADDIE

■ 1
● 58 black
○ 42 kiwi lime

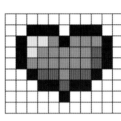

TiNY HEART

■ 1
● 20 black
◐ 7 magenta
● 16 bubblegum
○ 3 light pink

 1
◉ 15 pastel yellow
○ 15 pastel lavender
○ 15 prickly pear
◉ 9 cheddar
○ 9 toothpaste
◉ 18 orange
◉ 9 turquoise
○ 10 light green
● 10 plum
◉ 25 magenta

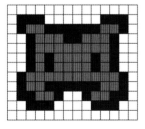

MAGENTA BADDIE

 1
● 50 black
◉ 48 magenta

Hair Clip: Glue a design to a sturdy hair clip for a cute accent you're sure to love. Make one in every color so you're always coordinated with your outfit!

Clips and Pins: Glue a small set of beads to the tip of a clothespin to brighten it up and make your office area super organized.

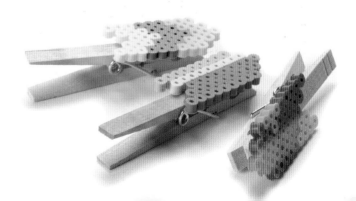

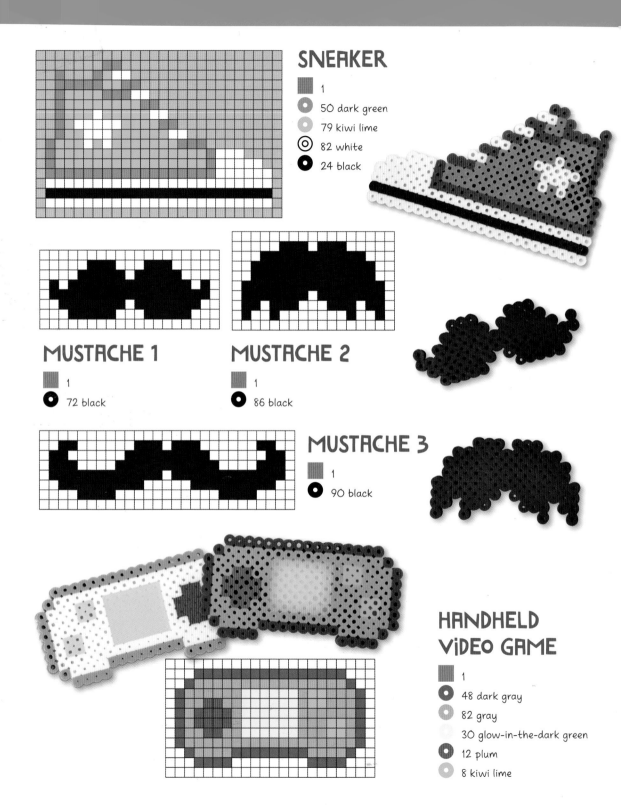

SNEAKER

- 1
- ◉ 50 dark green
- ◉ 79 kiwi lime
- ◉ 82 white
- ◉ 24 black

MUSTACHE 1

- 1
- ● 72 black

MUSTACHE 2

- 1
- ● 86 black

MUSTACHE 3

- 1
- ● 90 black

HANDHELD VIDEO GAME

- 1
- ◉ 48 dark gray
- ◉ 82 gray
- ◉ 30 glow-in-the-dark green
- ◉ 12 plum
- ◉ 8 kiwi lime

Drink Covers: These circular coasters have a hole in the center, so they can work double duty as drink covers. The hole is just large enough for your straw to fit through, so your drink will be protected from bugs during picnics and poolside lounging.

CHECKED DRINK COVER

 1

◎ 88 white

● 88 prickly pear

● 88 toothpaste

PINWHEEL DRINK COVER

● 1

● 45 hot coral

● 88 orange

● 88 cheddar

45 yellow

STRIPED DRINK COVER

● 1

● 54 plum

● 48 purple

● 78 pastel lavender

● 30 dark blue

● 42 turquoise

12 toothpaste

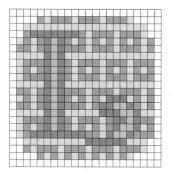

"L" LOVE COASTER

- ▦ 1
- ◌ 147 light pink
- ◍ 147 bubblegum
- ◍ 64 parrot green
- ◍ 22 light green

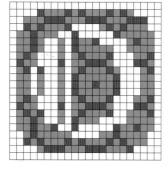

"O" LOVE COASTER

- ▦ 1
- ◍ 190 pastel lavender
- ◍ 89 purple
- ◎ 102 white

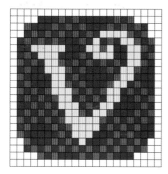

"V" LOVE COASTER

- ▦ 1
- ◍ 115 magenta
- ◍ 192 raspberry
- ◍ 73 light pink

Love Coasters: This matching set of four coasters makes a cheery statement for your guests and the eclectic colors really pop! Trace each coaster onto a piece of felt, cut out the felt, and glue the felt to the bottom of the coaster.

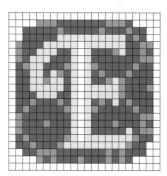

"E" LOVE COASTER

- ▦ 1
- ◍ 208 dark blue
- ◍ 66 turquoise
- ◍ 97 toothpaste
- ◎ 14 white

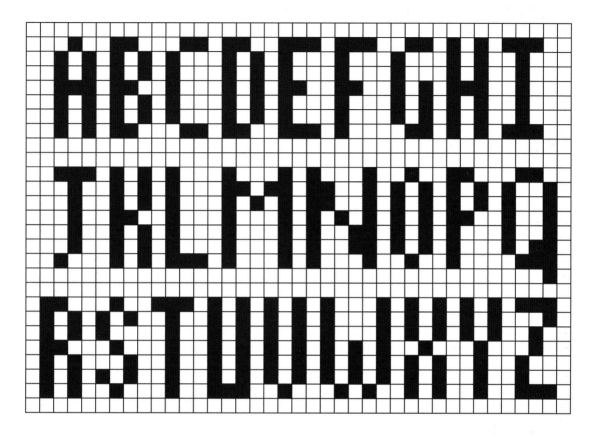

ALPHABET

Alphabet: Use these letters on any fusible bead project you can imagine!

PLANTER

Make a perfect little home for your favorite cactus or other green friend.
Even if you don't have a green thumb, your plant will be safe and secure.

Planter Bottom - Make 1

■	1
	261 crème
◉	269 plum
◎	311 pastel green

Planter Sides - Make 4

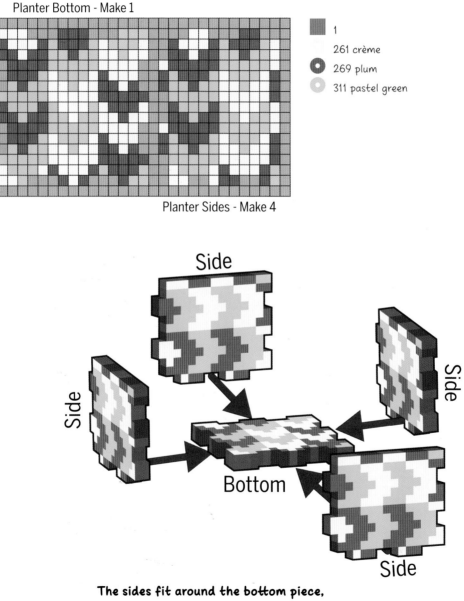

**The sides fit around the bottom piece,
forming a box without a top.**

To make the planter, iron all the pieces, but be sure not to iron the beads too long; you don't want them to flatten too much or they won't fit into one another. Iron them just enough to fuse them together. Then dab some hot glue into the nooks where the pieces join and attach them quickly. Join only a few nooks at a time and hold the pieces firmly together until the glue dries, which takes about 20–30 seconds.

tie-Dye

GENERAL TiE-DYE CRAFTING TiPS

Choosing Fibers

Tie-dyeing works best on natural fibers such as cotton, rayon, and hemp. Dye also works on silk, but the colors will sometimes shift or appear lighter. Synthetic fibers such as polyester fibers don't take dye very well, if at all.

Choosing Dyes

Look for fiber-reactive cold-water dyes that yield brilliant colors with excellent resistance to fading. They're simple to use and fairly safe. Always read the manufacturer's instructions carefully to ensure you're using the dye as effectively as possible. If your dye doesn't contain soda ash (check the packaging), you'll need to make a soda ash fixative solution to soak your garment in. Soda ash is mildly caustic, so wear gloves, safety goggles, and a dust mask when working with it, and only use it with adult supervision. In a large plastic bucket or tub, thoroughly dissolve one cup of soda ash in one gallon of water to create a solution. Use lower concentrations when working with young children or delicate fabrics, especially silk.

Basic Supplies

You'll need some combination of basic supplies to keep clean and work effectively. These might include: a plastic tablecloth, a plastic apron, plastic gloves, plastic wrap, paper towels, and plastic buckets or tubs.

Setting and Rinsing

Wrap the garment in plastic wrap to keep it damp (or put it in a plastic zip-top bag). Let it set for 4 to 24 hours to allow the dye to fix in the fibers. A longer setting time produces deeper colors. Rinse under running water until the water runs clear, then remove any bindings and rinse again. To remove any remaining dye, wash immediately according to the garment washing instructions. Make sure to wash your newly tie-dyed garments separately for the first few times.

CRUMPLE DYE

Crumple-dyeing is an easy way to dye fabric with subtle color changes and interesting visual texture. It is also the easiest technique and a great place to start. Simple technique; dazzling results!

MATERIALS

- Garment
- Soda ash fixative solution, if necessary
- Plastic tub or flat glass baking dish
- Applicator bottle(s)
- Dyes
- Basic supplies as needed

1. Soak the garment in water (or fixative, if necessary).
2. Spread it on a table and crumple it into a flat pancake shape with your glove-covered fingers (A). Transfer it to a plastic tub.
3. Apply dye with an applicator bottle in an all-over squiggle motion (B).
4. Carefully turn the garment over, keeping the existing crumples in place, and apply dye to the back of the garment in the same way.
5. Place the garment on a table, flatten it out, and crumple it again, bringing areas without dye to the top.
6. Dilute the dye remaining in the applicator bottle by refilling the bottle with water. Then repeat the crumple-dye process.
7. Let set and rinse.
8. To get even more interesting effects, dye a second time with a different color and a third time with a mixture of two colors, diluted dye, or three different colors.

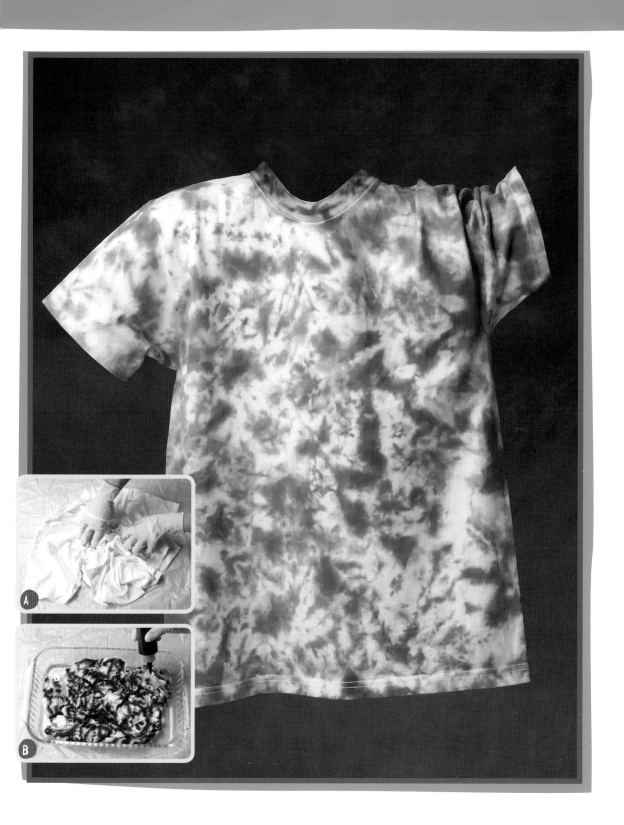

SUNBURSTS AND CiRCLES

Some of the oldest examples of tie-dyeing were created using techniques similar to this. Sunbursts and circles have a timeless appeal, but are fairly simple to create with some practice. Try your hand at this rainbow sunburst to get started.

MATERIALS

- Garment
- Rubber bands
- Soda ash fixative solution, if necessary
- Applicator bottle(s)
- Dyes
- Basic supplies as needed

1. Pinch the center of the sunburst and bind it with a rubber band about 2" (5cm) down (A). If you're dyeing a shirt, you may want to align the center of the sunburst with the bottom of the armholes, not the actual center of the front of the shirt.
2. Continue to gather and bind the shirt at 2" (5cm) intervals (B).
3. Soak the garment in water (or fixative, if necessary).
4. Use an applicator bottle to apply yellow dye to the first three sections (C). When you dye a sunburst design, be sure to inject dye down into thicker bound areas, because a lot of fabric is hiding in the folds.
5. Apply fuchsia dye to the second, third, and fourth sections. Then apply turquoise dye (D) to the fourth, fifth, and sixth sections.
6. Continue layering colors, creating orange, green, and purple, until you run out of fabric.
7. Let set and rinse.

DANDELION VARIATION

Make this variation by dyeing yellow down the folds and orange on the edges.

SWIRLS

When you think "tie-dye," you probably think of this design first. The rainbow swirl is a classic choice with tons of potential variations. The basic technique is simple, and the design can be varied in many ways depending on how colors are applied to the wedges.

MATERIALS

- Garment
- Large rubber bands
- Soda ash fixative solution, if necessary
- Applicator bottle(s)
- Dyes
- Basic supplies as needed

1. Place the garment flat and pinch a bit of fabric where you want the swirl (A). If you're dyeing a shirt, you may want to align the center of the swirl with the bottom of the armholes, not the actual center of the front of the shirt.
2. Pressing down, wind the garment into a flat swirl. Split the folds at the outside edges of the design (B).
3. Bind as shown with three rubber bands crossing in the center (C).
4. Soak the garment in water (or fixative, if necessary).
5. Apply yellow dye on three sections and half of the two adjacent sections (D).
6. Apply fuchsia dye on three sections, overlapping one section of yellow (E).
7. Apply turquoise dye on one section of fuchsia, one white section, and one yellow section (F).
8. Turn the garment over and dye the reverse side in same manner.
9. Let set and rinse.

GRAPHIC VARIATION

Make this variation by dyeing two wedges purple, the adjacent two wedges green, and leaving the remaining wedges white.

PLEATS

Pleated designs can be simple, loose, unbound pleats for a subtle overall effect, or they can be the basis for a striking multicolored design. Pleating along a curved or slanted line creates an interesting variation. Draw a line with a fabric pencil, then stack the pleats carefully along the line.

MATERIALS

- Garment
- Large rubber bands
- Fabric pencil, if necessary
- Soda ash fixative solution, if necessary
- Applicator bottle(s)
- Dyes
- Basic supplies as needed

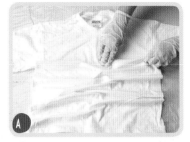

1. Soak the garment in water (or fixative, if necessary).
2. Place the garment flat and arrange in 2" (5cm) horizontal pleats broken in the middle (A). Use a fabric pencil line to help align the pleats, if necessary.
3. Fold the pleated garment in half.
4. Apply dye to the edges, leaving some white (B).
5. Turn the garment over and dye the reverse side in the same manner.
6. Let set and rinse.

ACROSS THE CHEST VARIATION

Make this variation by arranging vertical pleats across the chest and applying fuchsia and orange dye on the folds across the chest.

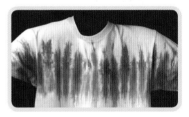

NECK VARIATION

1. Mark dots about 4" (10cm) from the collar with a fabric pencil. Draw a line to connect the dots.
2. Pleat the garment on the line and place one rubber band over the line and another about 3" (7.5cm) lower.
3. Apply yellow dye and then fuchsia dye between the rubber bands, letting the colors overlap.
4. Apply turquoise dye near the collar section.
5. Wrap the rainbow section with plastic wrap.
6. Dye the rest of the shirt in a bowl with diluted turquoise dye until the color is smooth.

Duct tape

GENERAL DUCT TAPE CRAFTING TIPS

For the projects in this book, you'll need to be able to make two-sided sheets of duct tape. This method creates finished edges that are folded over so the whole piece looks polished.

1. Stick a strip of duct tape slightly longer than needed on your cutting mat (sticky side down). Overlap one long edge of the first strip by about ¼"—½" (0.5—1.5cm) with a second strip. Continue until you have a rectangle of tape slightly larger than required for your project. This will be the back of your sheet.

2. When all the strips are in place, trim the sheet so it's the exact size you need. Flip it over so the sticky side is facing up.

3. Apply strips of tape to the sticky side of the sheet just like in step 1. Place the strips so they extend past the edges of the sheet by about ½" (1.5cm) or so on all sides. This will be the front of your sheet.

4. Flip the sheet over so the back side is facing up. Using scissors, trim the corners of the exposed sticky portion, cutting close to the back corners without actually cutting into them. If you want to leave some sides cleanly cut instead of folded over, simply trim them off here.

5. Fold over the exposed sticky edges to the back of the sheet to create a clean finish. If desired, you can use the sticky edges to attach your sheet to another piece instead of folding them over!

To give your sheet some extra thickness, you can add cardboard! Cut a piece of cardboard to the exact size you need. In step 1, cover the cardboard with tape on one side. Then, in step 2, trim the excess tape from the edges of the cardboard. Follow steps 3—5 as before.

CHARGING CADDY

Cut an empty bottle of lotion in half with an extension in the back. Cut a hole in the extension large enough for your charging plug, then wrap the whole package in duct tape. Your phone now has a place to rest while it charges!

GAMING SYSTEM

Create your own custom gaming station by decorating your console and controllers in duct tape.

CUSTOM KICKS

Create a stand-out sticker for your favorite pair of sneakers.

CHAIN JEWELRY

Cut 3" (7.5cm) lengths of ¼" (0.5cm)-diameter cording and wrap each piece with duct tape. Connect the ends to form links. Join the links together as you make them to create cool chain jewelry pieces.

HOME TEAM BALL

Cover your favorite sports equipment in duct tape and give your team the edge.

DUCT TAPE WALLET

This handy wallet holds cash and your ID and even has a few slots for cards. It's the perfect and classic wallet with a twist. Decorate it however you like!

MATERIALS

- Duct tape in 2–3 colors
- 4" x 2½" (10 x 6.5cm) piece of report cover plastic
- Craft knife
- Cutting mat

1. Follow the instructions on page 148 to make three double-sided sheets in the following sizes: one 9" x 6½" (23 x 16.5cm), two 4" x 2" (10 x 5cm). Follow the pattern diagrams below.

2. Measure down 3⅜" (8.5cm) from one long edge of the wallet. Then fold the wallet lengthwise along this line. One side should be slightly higher than the other; this will be the bill slot once both ends are taped.

3. Fold a ½" (1.5cm)-wide strip of duct tape in half over one long end of your ID pocket piece.

4. Place the ID pocket piece on the inner side of your wallet, aligning the right and bottom edges. Tape the pocket in place along the sides and bottom with ½" (1.5cm)-wide strips of tape. Tape around the entire right end of the wallet as you do this to finish one end of the bill slot.

5. Align the left edge of one card pocket with the left edge of the wallet, about ¾" (2cm) down from the top edge. Tape the pocket in place along the bottom edge only. Attach the second pocket ½" (1.5cm) down from the first, now taping along the sides and bottom. Tape around the entire left end of the wallet as you do this to finish the left end of the bill slot. Use more ½" (1.5cm)-wide strips of tape to decorate the front of the wallet.

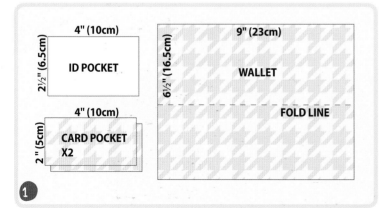

4" (10cm)
2½" (6.5cm)
ID POCKET

4" (10cm)
2" (5cm)
CARD POCKET X2

9" (23cm)
6½" (16.5cm)
WALLET
FOLD LINE

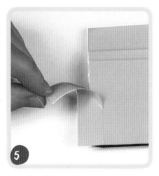

DUCT TAPE WRIST CUFF

Water bottles are everywhere, it seems, and they pile up faster than you can recycle them. So why not upcycle a few into awesome wrist cuffs? They look great with a bit of added decoration—like brads as faux studs—and fit everybody!

MATERIALS

- Duct tape
- Small water bottle (14—18 oz.)
- Brads
- Cutting mat
- Craft knife

1. Cut off the top and bottom of your water bottle, leaving just the center flat portion. Start by cutting a slit with your craft knife, then trim off the ends with scissors. You will be left with a tube of plastic.

2. Cut the tube open so you can slide the cuff on and off your wrist. Round off the cut edges with scissors.

3. To cover the plastic cuff, you have two options. The first is to use a sheet of duct tape. Lay out the sheet (sticky side up). Then center the cuff on top and flatten it out to each side smoothly. Finish the edges as described on page 148. Repeat to cover the other side.

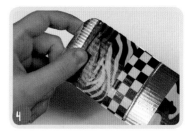

4. Alternatively, you can use several strips placed vertically over the cuff to cover the area with more ease and create an interesting striped effect.

5. Poke holes in the cuff with your craft knife and install brads as desired. Remember to cover the prongs with more tape when finished.

DUCT TAPE SKETCHBOOK

No special skills necessary—this book-binding technique requires nothing but duct tape! Create a sketchbook with your favorite drawing paper, or use whatever paper you want to make a book suited to your purposes.

MATERIALS

- Duct tape
- Sheets of filler paper of your choosing
- Heavy cardboard: two squares ⅛" (0.3cm) wider and ¼" (0.5cm) longer than your paper sheets
- Cutting mat
- Craft knife

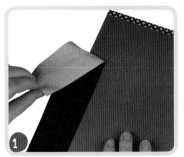

1. Take one sheet of paper and layer a strip of duct tape over the edge you want to be along the spine. Place the duct tape lengthwise along the edge so half of it extends out past the paper.

2. Flip the paper over so the sticky side of the tape is up. Attach the next sheet, butting it against the first so it covers the exposed half of the tape. Trim any excess tape at the top and bottom.

3. Fold the pages in half along the center seam so the tape is on the inside. Repeat steps 1–3 to continue creating sheets until you're happy with the amount.

4. Cover the cardboard pieces with tape (as you would make a double-sided sheet). Repeat steps 1–3 to attach the front cover to the top sheet in the stack of paper. Attach the back cover to the bottom sheet in the stack. When finished, apply more strips of tape down the spine to cover it and help hold the cardboard pieces in place.

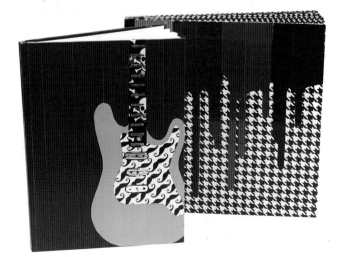

DUCT TAPE LUGGAGE TAG

This handy holder is a perfect fit for tagging your luggage or for just running out the door with your ID in hand.

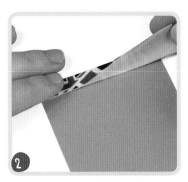

MATERIALS

- Duct tape
- 3" x 4½" (7.5 x 11.5cm) piece of cardboard
- 2½" x 3¾" (6.5 x 9.5cm) piece of report cover plastic
- 1 brad
- Cutting mat
- Craft knife

1. Trim the corners of your cardboard piece so they are rounded. Then cover both sides with tape (as you would make a double-sided sheet). Make a strap that is 10" (25.5cm) long for a wrist strap or 30" (76cm) long for a neck strap. To make a strap, take a strip of duct tape and fold under both edges, using a ruler to keep the line straight. Follow the pattern diagrams below.

2. Fold a ½" (1.5cm)-wide strip of duct tape in half over one short end of your pocket piece.

3. Center the pocket on top of the base, aligning the bottom edges. Then tape it in place along the sides and bottom using ½" (1.5cm)-wide strips of duct tape.

4. Using your craft knife, cut a rectangular hole measuring ⅛" x ¾" (0.3 x 2cm) about ¼" (0.5cm) down from the top edge of the holder.

5. Loop the strap through the hole in the base and secure the ends with duct tape. Install a brad going through the strap for more security, and then cover the exposed prongs on the back side with more duct tape.

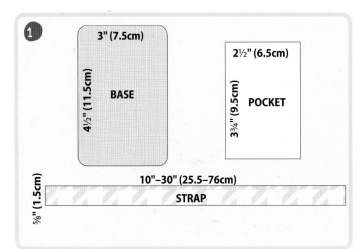

INDEX

Vacation Crafting is a collection of new and previously published material. Portions of this book have been reproduced from *Awesome Duct Tape Projects* (ISBN 978-1-57421-895-4), *Awesome Foam Craft* (ISBN 978-1-57421-352-2), *Best of Seashells* (ISBN 978-1-57421-330-0), *Big Bold Beads* (ISBN 978-1-57421-328-7), *Epic Rubber Band Crafts* (ISBN 978-1-57421-914-2), *Foam and Glitter* (ISBN 978-1-57421-316-4), *Friendship Bracelets 101* (ISBN 978-1-57421-212-9), *Friendship Bracelets All Grown Up* (ISBN 978-1-57421-866-4), *Hemp It Up with Beads* (ISBN 978-1-57421-147-4), *Hemp Jewelry* (ISBN 978-1-5048-0015-0), *Hip Hemp with Beads* (ISBN 978-1-57421-265-5), *Lanyards A-Z* (ISBN 978-1-57421-291-4), *Pixel Craft with Perler Beads* (ISBN 978-1-57421-993-7), *Plastic Lace Crafts for Beginners* (ISBN 978-1-57421-367-6), *Strings 'n Things* (ISBN 978-1-57421-293-8), and *Totally Awesome Tie-Dye* (ISBN 978-1-4972-0369-3). Reproduction of its contents is strictly prohibited without written permission from the rights holder. All content is copyright its respective owners and published by Fox Chapel Publishing Company, Inc.

Step-by-step photography for duct tape projects (pages 148, 150, 152, 154, and 156) and fusible bead projects (pages 130 and 139) by Matthew McClure. Photos on pages 151 and 153 by Eric Forberger. Shutterstock images: page 13 top photo frame image by Sergey Novikov; page 13 bottom photo frame image by Sergey Nivens.

ISBN 978-1-64124-017-8

The Cataloging-in-Publication Data in on file with the Library of Congress.

To learn more about the other great books from Fox Chapel Publishing, or to find a retailer near you, call toll-free 800-457-9112 or visit us at *www.FoxChapelPublishing.com*.

We are always looking for talented authors. To submit an idea, please send a brief inquiry to acquisitions@foxchapelpublishing.com.

Printed in Singapore
First printing

ABOUT THE CONTRIBUTORS

Suzanne McNeill: Suzanne McNeill is the author of 230 craft & hobby books, and her creative vision has placed her books on top of the trends for over 25 years. Winner of the Craft and Hobby Association's Industry Achievement Award, Suzanne has been called "the Trendsetter" of the arts and crafts industry. Dedicated to hands-on creativity, she constantly tests, experiments, and invents something new and fun.

Choly Knight: Choly Knight has her finger on the pulse of what today's young crafters really want. Choly has been crafting for as long as she can remember, and has drawn, painted, sculpted, and taped everything in sight. A power-seller on Etsy, she is the author of six terrific craft books from Fox Chapel Publishing. Choly enjoys combining all her passions of writing, fine art, craft art, and design, as she provides techniques, tutorials, and excitement for her many readers and fans. You can find out more about her and her work on her website: *www. cholyknight.com.*

David Kominz, Phyllis Damon, David Hall: Phyllis Damon began her career teaching weaving and supplying craft materials in educational settings. David Kominz, a retired NIH medical researcher, joined forces with Phyllis in the creation and publication of craft books. Together with master designer of plastic lacing, David Hall, they turned out three plastic lacing books. Their goal has been to help kids have fun and develop creativity through basic craft skills.

Margaret Riley: A veteran of the craft industry, Margaret Riley has owned and operated two hobby and craft stores and created many craft projects in addition to serving as a designer, editor, manufacturer consultant, demonstrator, and teacher. Her favorite fields include oil painting, acrylics, watercolors, charcoal, pencil, pen and ink, calligraphy, decorative painting, landscapes, scrapbooking, rubber stamping, paper creations, clay, general crafts, sewing, quilting, jewelry, knitting, crocheting, crewel, cross stitching, and embroidery.

Colleen Dorsey: Colleen Dorsey is a writer specializing in the craft and hobby industry, and an editor at Fox Chapel Publishing. Colleen has edited books on many topics, including foam and paper crafts, jewelry making, and children's crafts. She graduated from Johns Hopkins University with a degree in creative writing, and in her spare time she enjoys writing fiction, making jewelry, and upcycling findings into crafty new items.

Andrea Gibson: Andrea Gibson designs jewelry, layouts, and cards and teaches at shops, workshops, and scrapbook shows.

Janie Ray: Janie Ray is a native of Fort Worth, Texas, and enjoys patchwork, beading, gardening, and knotting hemp.